Luther's Scottish Connection

Luther's Scottish Connection

James Edward McGoldrick

Rutherford • Madison • Teaneck
Fairleigh Dickinson University Press
London and Toronto: Associated University Presses

Associated University Presses
440 Forsgate Drive
Cranbury, NJ 08512

Associated University Presses
25 Sicilian Avenue
London WC1A 2QH, England

Associated University Presses
P.O. Box 488, Port Credit
Mississauga, Ontario
Canada L5G 4M2

The paper used in this publication meets the requirements
of the American National Standard for Permanence of Paper
for Printed Library Materials Z39.48-1984.

Library of Congress Cataloging-in-Publication Data

McGoldrick, James Edward.
    Luther's Scottish connection / James Edward McGoldrick.
    p.   cm.
    Bibliography: p.
    Includes index.
    ISBN 0-8386-3357-9 (alk. paper)
    1. Reformation—Scotland.   2. Lollards.   3. Lutheran Church-
-Scotland—History—16th century.   4. Luther, Martin, 1483–1546-
-Influence.   5. Scotland—Church history—16th century.   I. Title.
BR385.M36   1989
274.11′06-dc19   88-46054
                                                                       CIP

PRINTED IN THE UNITED STATES OF AMERICA

Contents

Preface   7
Acknowledgments   9

1   Scotland in the Late Middle Ages   13
2   Scotland in the Renaissance   27
3   The Rise of Scottish Protestantism   33
4   Scotland's Earliest Protestants   55
5   Conclusion   70

Appendix   74
Notes   101
Annotated Bibliography   110
Index   121
About the Author   123

Preface

There is no doubt whatever that the Protestant Reformation in Scotland received its principal direction from the indomitable John Knox, a rigorous and courageous adherent to the Reformed version of evangelical teaching as espoused in Geneva by John Calvin and his disciples. The stature of Knox looms large over the Scottish church and rightly so, for his contributions to its reformation were major and decisive. It is highly unlikely that the movement to reform that church could have succeeded without Knox, or at least without a leader of his conspicuous ability. Any serious examination of the Reformation in Scotland must therefore acknowledge his monumental importance.

Although even those who have only a casual acquaintance with Scottish history usually have some appreciation for the significance of Knox, few seem to realize that he was not literally the father of the Reformation in his homeland. There were several precursors of Knox who laid the foundations upon which he built, and those forerunners were, for the most part, disciples of Martin Luther. It is the purpose of this book to identify the most prominent Scottish Lutherans and to relate the roles they played in the first phase of Scotland's Protestant history.

The author makes no claim to originality. His objective is to bring together in one place information that heretofore has appeared only in articles and as relatively minor emphases in books narrating the Scottish Reformation. It has been well over a hundred years since anyone has published a book dealing at length and in a systematic manner with the Lutheran phase of the Reformation in Scotland, and even then some of the figures who appear in the present volume received only slight attention.

The present author has examined most of the primary sources employed by previous writers on this subject and has found that his predecessors have, for the most part, understood them well and used them appropriately. I am therefore indebted to all of them, and I hope that I have done them justice in drawing upon their learning. The decision about which early Protestants to include in this study and the interpretations expressed and implied are, of course, my own. Although a few other personalities from the first half of the sixteenth century might have been included, those who do appear in this book were selected because, in my judgment, they were all important links in the chain of Luther's Scottish connection.

Acknowledgments

The decision to write this book came in response to a suggestion from Pastor Bruce W. Adams, Jr., of St. James Evangelical Lutheran Church, Moorabbin, Victoria, Australia. Mr. Adams had read my earlier work, *Luther's English Connection*, with great appreciation, and he suggested that I examine the manner in which Luther's influence reached Scotland and helped to shape the contours of the early Protestant Reformation there. For his encouragement and kind assistance with the project I shall always be grateful.

Thanks are due to Vice-President Clifford W. Johnson and Professor J. Murray Murdoch of Cedarville College, who obtained faculty development funds to pay for the production of the manuscript; to Miss Gina Long, who did the actual typing; and to Mr. and Mrs. Donald Johnson, who typed the appendix and reproduced the manuscript on a laser printer. The staff of the Cedarville College Library was always very helpful, especially in arranging interlibrary loans, and a special word of gratitude goes to Miss Barbara Yanda, who handled most of my numerous requests for materials from other libraries. She frequently went beyond the call of duty to help me.

Finally, I owe a substantial debt to Professor W. Stanford Reid of the University of Guelph, Ontario. A distinguished authority on the Scottish Reformation himself, Professor Reid read the manuscript and made valuable suggestions to improve it.

Luther's Scottish Connection

1

Scotland in the Late Middle Ages

Although Protestantism in its Calvinistic or Reformed ex-
pression achieved almost total victory in Scotland in the sixteenth
century, the northern kingdom of Britain was a stronghold of
Roman Catholicism through most of medieval history. In their
struggle to be free from English interference, however, the Scots
became fiercely nationalistic and therefore somewhat resistant
toward the political policies of the Papacy. Motivated by royal or
baronial greed, the Scots enacted numerous laws to restrict papal
prerogatives in their land. Such laws were sometimes intended to
enhance the opportunity to acquire ecclesiastical revenues. Papal
support for England during the period of Anglo-Scottish strife
aroused considerable dislike for Rome, and, during the era of the
Great Schism (1378–1417), when rival popes in Rome and Avignon contended for supremacy over the church, Scotland and
England took opposite sides.

In order to gain effective control over lucrative church offices
and properties, secular lords in Scotland sought to curtail the
pope's authority. Since the Papacy had been weakened and somewhat discredited by the Great Schism, the Scots had a fine opportunity to pursue this design. In 1426 the parliament of Scotland
forbade clergymen from seeking benefices from Rome. When
King James I (1406–37) decided that he could not extract useful
concessions from Popes Martin V (1417–31) and Eugene IV
(1431–47), the monarch gave his support to the Concil of Basel, a
general ecclesiastical body that Martin V had summoned shortly
before he died. Eugene IV found that he had inherited a re-
bellious council that he could not control. The king of Scotland's
willingness to support a council critical of the pope reflects James's
determination to secure ecclesiastical autonomy for his kingdom.

13

As the fifteenth century unfolded, additional antipapal measures were enacted into law in Scotland. In 1482, for example, Parliament granted to the archbishop of St. Andrews the right to confirm monastic authorities in their offices without approval from Rome. Although antipapal laws were neither enacted nor enforced with consistency, such legislation was common through the century. By the early sixteenth century the Scots had largely achieved the degree of independence from Rome for which their kings and lords had been striving for about a century.[1]

The church over which the kings of Scotland desired to secure control was strongly Catholic in doctrine, and the monarchs intended to keep it that way. While they wanted to distance themselves from Roman authority, they had no desire to remove Scotland from the fold of the universal church, and the maintenance of Catholic orthodoxy was a prominent royal concern. This had become evident in the fourteenth century, when heresy made its debut in the land. In 1329 Pope John XXII, who reigned at Avignon, issued a bull that directed the rulers of Scotland to extirpate heresy. The pope declared that he would withold the traditional anointing of the king if he did not implement the Vatican's decree against religious nonconformity. For the most part such threats were not necessary, because the kings were intent upon preserving the Catholic character of their state anyway.

The precise origins of heresy in Scotland are rather obscure, but by the early fifteenth century the teachings of England's John Wycliffe were exerting a significant influence there. Wycliffe (ca. 1328–84), a professor of theology at Oxford University, was a highly learned scholar who had been influenced by the writings of the church father St. Augustine (354–430). Through his reading of Augustinian treatises and his personal study of the Bible, Wycliffe came to believe that the church in his day had drifted far from its apostolic foundations, both in doctrine and in practice. He sought therefore to reform in church in accord with his understanding of Scripture. This led him to deny papal claims to spiritual and temporal supremacy over Christendom and to assert the independence of the king of England in all affairs of state.

Wycliffe's deviations from the doctrinal standards of medieval orthodoxy included a rejection of transubstantiation, the teaching

14

that the bread and wine of the Eucharist become the actual body and blood of Christ when consecrated by a priest in the sacrifice of the Mass. He held that the true church is the body of God's elect from all ages, and that it is not identical with the ecclesiastical organization formally called the Catholic church. Wycliffe was incensed over the material and political preoccupations of some popes, and eventually he called the papacy the "damned limbs of Lucifer," that is, Antichrist.

The influence of St. Augustine is particularly clear in Wycliffe's teaching about salvation. The English reformer held to *sola gratia,* the belief that salvation is a gift of pure grace that God bestows upon his chosen people. This contrasted sharply with the view then prevalent that salvation is a synergistic process through which believers earn eternal life by performing works of righteousness made possible by grace.

Although the medieval church was threatened by Wycliffe's nonconformity in matters of doctrine, his pointed attacks upon clerical corruption and abuses may have aroused even more ecclesiastical animosity. He maintained that the church had become corrupt through its alliance with and reliance upon civil authorities. Although this relationship had brought great wealth and influence, it had, in Wycliffe's judgment, distracted the church and its clergy from their spiritual responsibilities. As a remedy he proposed that clergymen be excluded from civil positions, that the church be deprived of the right to collect tithes compulsorily, and that bishops and priests be forced to live on offerings given freely by the people. Wycliffe wanted clergymen to give priority to preaching as a means to instruct their congregations in biblical doctrine in order to promote a revival of piety in the land. Since most priests in England at that time seldom preached, this was a revolutionary proposal.[2]

In order to advance his plan for ecclesiastical reform, Wycliffe believed it essential to translate the Bible into English and to place it in the hands of clerics who would then teach it to the people. It is not known for certain exactly how much of the translation was done by Wycliffe himself. He may have done the New Testament, while his associate Nicholas Hereford rendered the Old Testament into English. In any case, the translations from the Vulgate were completed by 1384. A revised edition appeared about 1388.

Despite the lack of any means for mass reproduction, the Lollard Bible, as Wycliffe's version became known, enjoyed considerable circulation, and more than one hundred copies are extant.[3]

For reasons not at all clear, the followers of John Wycliffe were known as Lollards, and by the early fifteenth century these "poor priests" ("mumblers," as they were sometimes called in derision) were active in Scotland, especially in the lowlands. The area south of Glasgow seems to have been a pocket of strength for the movement.[4] The extent of Lollard activity in Scotland is uncertain, because records of the Scottish bishoprics from that time are extremely fragmentary. This makes it difficult to know exactly how Wycliffe's teachings were carried to the northern kingdom, but Oxford University was a likely point of contact, for a number of Scots studied there. Although documentary evidence about Scottish students at Oxford is scant, it is clear that those who went there were in a position to absorb Wycliffe's ideas. Henry Wardlaw, who became bishop of St. Andrews in 1402, was educated at Oxford and went on to assist in the founding of Scotland's first university at St. Andrews. One ancient account relates that St. Andrews University was established as an institution to combat heresy. In 1416 that school decreed that all masters of arts had to denounce Lollardy and swear to uphold the Catholic faith.[5]

That Lollardy had become a serious challenge to Catholic authorities sometime before the opening of St. Andrews University is evident. The first reference to the Lollards in Scotland comes from Andrew of Wyntoun, canon of St. Andrews, who had become prior to St. Serf's monastery about 1395. Wyntoun's *Original Chronicle,* which he completed about 1420, is a vital primary source for the study of this era. In praising the duke of Albany for his strong profession of religion. Wyntoun remarked, "In all tym rycht devote, he was a constant Catholike; all Lollard he hatyt and heretike."[6]

Wyntoun entered the above remark in his chronicle in 1406, which shows that Wycliffe's doctrine had reached Scotland at an early date. Since Lollards were persecuted in England soon after Wycliffe's death, some may have fled north as refugees who carried his message as they went. In fact, it is possible that Lollardy was present there as early as 1402, for in that year the English bishop of Durham wrote to the monks of Kelso to seek their aid in apprehending three clerics of unorthodox beliefs who were be-

16

lieved to have fled to Scotland.[7] Evidently, the first Lollard in Scotland to suffer martyrdom was James Resby, an English priest and disciple of Wycliffe, who was executed at Perth in 1407. Resby was examined by Laurence of Lindores, inquisitor of heretical pravity, for forty offenses against the Catholic faith. The only charges that have been verified are that he denied that the pope is the vicar of Christ on earth, and that he contended that personal holiness is prerequisite for one who occupies the papal throne. The indictment depicts Resby as a Wycliffite, and it indicates that others in Scotland held to the same teachings. Among the charges brought against Resby, it is clear that his rejection of papal authority and his contention that the clergy had no control over the dispensation of divine grace were the most damning. The Lollards relied on preaching as the principal means of spreading their message, and it appears that Resby functioned in Scotland as a Lollard evangelist. Scottish Lollards denied the sacramental character of penance that involved oral confession of sins to a priest, a rejection that was a prominent feature of Wycliffe's doctrine.[8]

The next Scottish Lollard who can be identified by name was Quentin Folkhyrde, author of some letters sent from Scotland to Bohemia in 1410. This correspondence appears to be typically Lollard in content in that it contains strongly worded complaints about clerical laxity and corruption and calls for priests to study the Bible, to preach its truths in the vernacular tongue, and to administer the sacraments without charge. The author claimed that his quest for the reform of the church was his moral responsibility, and he feared the loss of salvation if he failed to pursue it.

Folkhyrde's call for reform was pointedly anticlerical. He called upon nobles and commoners to remove incorrigible priests, and he warned that those who tolerated evil clerics would share their guilt before God. In the second letter Folkhyrde said that nobles had a duty "to be acquainted with the law of God and to defend it, to protect the servants of Christ, and to crush the agents of Antichrist, . . . for this is the reason for their carrying the sword."[9]

In his letters (known collectively as *Nova Scocie*) Folkhyrde did not seek schism in the church, but his blunt criticisms of the clergy provoked strong opposition. He indicated that churchmen who felt threatened by his attacks had tried to enlist secular lords to repress him. He said that he would, if necessary, sacrifice his life rather than be silent. His appeals fell on unresponsive ears, and no mention of Folkhyrde has been found in the literature after 1410. What happened to him is not known, but Lollardy continued to gain strength in Scotland, as the decision of St. Andrews in 1416 to require all masters of arts to oppose it bears witness. In 1420 several heretics were seized in Scotland for teaching Wycliffe's doctrines.[10]

Although Folkhyrde's precise connection with Bohemia has not been established, he did travel in England, where he had opportunities to meet Lollards, and perhaps it was there that he contacted people who had relations with Bohemia. By that time John Huss was waging a struggle to reform the church in his country along the same lines as those of Wycliffe and the Lollards in England and Scotland. In 1383 the English king Richard II had married Princess Anna of Bohemia, and after that Czech students began to study at Oxford University, from which they took Wycliffe's doctrines and writings to their homeland. The University of Prague then became a center of interest in the teachings of the English heretic, and John Huss (ca. 1373–1415) became leader of a movement that resembled Lollardy rather closely. The English influence at Prague was reinforced further when Peter Payne, principal of St. Edmund's Hall. Oxford, went there as a refugee from persecution at home and joined the Czech faculty of theology, where he became a leading Hussite scholar.

Whatever may have been the Scottish contribution to the Hussite movement, it is evident that Bohemia exerted some influence on the development of Lollardy in Scotland. In 1433 Paul Craw (or Crawar) appeared in St. Andrews as an emissary from Bohemia who aspired to communicate his theological beliefs to scholars and students at Scotland's only university. Craw was a learned man, a physician who had served the king of Bohemia. He went to St. Andrews, probably because he knew that town had shown some receptivity to Lollard teachings. There he had the misfortune of falling into the clutches of Laurence of Lindores, the inquisitor who had condemned James Resby earlier. Craw was accused of the following offenses: placing the Bible in the hands of the laity; denying the benefit of clergy, by which churchmen were exempt from prosecution in civil courts; and rejecting traditional church teachings on purgatory, Petrine succession in the papacy, priestly absolution in the sacrament of penance, and transubstantiation in the Eucharist. He and those who had become his disciples were charged also with denying the final resurrection of the dead at Christ's return and were said to have advocated community of goods and to have lived immorally. The accusations of lewdness made against them were probably without foundation, a means to slander them and thereby to enlarge the indictment against them.[11] Craw was executed, and according to the account given by John Knox, a brass ball was forced into his mouth when he was tied to the stake for burning.[12] There is no record that any others were burned with Craw.

Although information about heretics such as Resby, Folkhyrde, and Craw is distressingly meager, the eagerness of civil and ecclesiastical authorities to cooperate in suppressing religious nonconformity appears to indicate that Lollardy enjoyed a considerable following in the land. In 1424 the Parliament of Scotland enacted legislation to support the church authorities in the prosecution of heresy, which is evidence that the government regarded the Lollards as a serious threat.[13] The law declared that civil authorities were to support the church in the apprehension and punishment of heretics, specifically, Lollards.

Further evidence that Lollardy was a growing phenomenon in Scotland as the fifteenth century moved on may be seen in the founding of St. Salvatore's College at St. Andrews in 1450. This was the work of James Kennedy, bishop of St. Andrews, who intended this school to be an institution that would prepare clerics for the defense of the Catholic faith and the refutation of heresy. Pope Pius II (1458–64), who is often remembered under the name Aeneas Silvius, because of his achievements as a humanist scholar before he became pontiff, assisted Bishop Kennedy financially by granting a plenary indulgence to all who contributed toward maintaining and expanding St. Salvatore's College. To qualify for this spiritual benefit, subscribers had to confess their sins to a priest and perform nine days of penance. In return for their contrition, confessions, and contributions, they were promised "plenary absolution and remission, . . . for all sins, crimes, and excesses, even in cases [reserved] for the Apostolic See [Rome]." The income realized from this sale of indulgences was to be divided, one-third to go to Rome, and two-thirds to be used for the benefit of St. Salvatore's College.[14]

In 1469 Pope Paul II authorized St. Salvatore's College to confer master's degrees in arts and theology. At that point it was able to compete with St. Andrews University.

After the death of Paul Craw in 1433 there must have been significant heretical activity in Scotland, as the establishment of St. Salvatore's College bears witness. The evidence in hand, however, does not allow the verification of such activity until near the end of the fifteenth century, when thirty Lollards of Kyle and Cunningham in Ayrshire were apprehended and indicted before King James IV, his royal council, and Archbishop Blacader of Glasgow.

By 1494, when these people were arrested, Lollardy appears to have become a movement of laymen. Of the thirty people cited for heresy, the names of six have been preserved, and four of them were significant landowners—George Campbell of Cessnock, Adam Reid of Barskimming, John Campbell of Newmilns, and Andrew Shaw of Polkemmet. The other two, Helen Chalmers, Lady Polkellie, and Marion Chalmers, Lady Stair, were women of social standing.[15] The unnamed twenty-four could have been servants or relatives of the six.[16] The specific charges against the Lollards of Kyle were listed by Knox as, among others,

1. rejection of all use of images and relics in worship;
2. denial of Petrine succession and apostolic succession of papal authority;
3. contention that priests have no power to consecrate bread and wine, and that the eucharistic elements are not changed in the Mass;
4. refusal to pay tithes to the clergy;
5. assertion that all believers are priests;
6. rejection of indulgences, prayers and masses for the dead, as well as swearing oaths, prayers to the Virgin, and the authority of the church fathers;
7. assertion that the pope is Antichrist and that ecclesiastical authorities are thieves and robbers.[17]

Knox's account implies that the accused were acquitted, apparently because the king was disposed to be generous toward them. The monarch evidently knew them, an indication that they came from influential families. In the words of historian P. Hume

Brown, "Fortunately for the thirty heretics, the young king in whose presence they were examined was not of the stuff of which inquisitors are made, and he good-naturedly contrived to end the trial in a jest."[18]

The king's rather jocular attitude toward the Lollards of Kyle would seem to confirm the contention of Knox that the charge that they denied the king's right to judge in matters of religion was false. Had the accusation been legitimate, James IV would not have dismissed it so lightly. Knox concluded that the indictment was fabricated by people who wished to discredit the Lollard faith and to represent it as a subversive doctrine, and it seems that he was right.[19]

Like their counterparts in England, the Lollards of Scotland were eager to circulate the Bible in the vernacular language as widely as possible. Wycliffe's Bible as revised in 1388 by John Purvey became the basis for a New Testament version in the Scottish dialect by Murdoch Nisbet, who became a Lollard about 1500, In 1513 he went to Germany as a refugee, and there he obtained Purvey's rendition of the New Testament.[20] He later added a prologue that resembles closely Luther's preface to the German New Testament. In fact, Nisbet's translation/paraphrase may have been copied from Luther's work.[21]

Nisbet's contribution to the effort to make the scriptures available in vulgar tongues was, however, slight. His version of the New Testament was not printed, and the almost concurrent appearance of William Tyndale's New Testament in English prevented it from gaining wide acceptance. Until the advent of the Tyndale version, Scots had to depend on the Vulgate, which most of them could not read. An English-language Bible was fully comprehensible to literate Scots in the early sixteenth century, and the terms *Scottis* and *Inglis* were used without distinction by midcentury to denote the common language in Scotland. There were no major obstacles in written communication between Scots and Englishmen.[22]

During the Middle Ages the Roman Catholic church did not deny the supreme authority of Scripture. In fact, it was not until the Council of Trent (1563) that the church dogmatized the belief that ecclesiastical tradition is of equal authority with the Bible. The medieval church, however, did not encourage the production of vernacular translations of the Scriptures, although some portions in the common tongues did appear in various liturgical books by the fifteenth century. The hierarchy discouraged the use of vernacular translations on the assumption that laymen could not understand the real meaning of Scripture in any language, and laymen who possessed vernacular Bibles were sometimes suspected of heresy. Interest in the reading of the Bible grew despite official opposition. Not only heretical groups but movements within the Roman church produced versions in the spoken tongues. Several German Bibles appeared prior to publication of the *Deutsche Bibel*, Luther's masterpiece.

In medieval Scotland Catholics acquired some knowledge of the Bible from the sermons of the preaching friars—the Dominicans and the Franciscans—but clergymen as a whole were unlearned and therefore unable to expound the Scriptures to the people. The Lollards proposed to bring knowledge of the Bible to the common people through preaching, but they had no means for effecting the mass distribution of the Scriptures, because the printing press was not yet available to them. Lollard zeal in disseminating the teachings of the Bible reflects Lollard adherence to the principle of *sola scriptura*—the belief that the Bible is the supreme authority for the Christian life. English Lollards sought specific biblical warrants for all ecclesiastical practices, and it is highly probable that their Scottish counterparts did the same.[23]

The English New Testament in manuscript was being used by some Scots during the reign of James IV (1488–1513). John Campbell, laird of Cessnock, employed a priest to read the New Testament to him and his family. When the Campbells were accused of heresy for this practice, the king dismissed the charge. He was impressed especially by Mrs. Campbell's ability to argue on the basis of Scripture.[24] Since King James died in 1513, this must have happened quite a few years before the arrival of Tyndale's English New Testament, which did not appear in print until 1526. Copies of Tyndale's version began arriving in Scotland about the same time that they appeared in England, and the Scriptures were smuggled into both kingdoms from the Continent, where they had been printed.[25] The wholesale distribution of the Bible, which the Lollards would have dearly loved to accomplish, was reserved for the Protestants who succeeded them as advocates of *sola scriptura*.

In appraising the significance of Lollardy in Scotland it is clear that the evidence is much more useful in ascertaining what the Lollards opposed than what they actually believed. There were no noteworthy theologians comparable to Wycliffe among them, and the exact degree to which they may have adhered to or deviated from his teachings cannot be known. It is evident, however, that the Lollards in both British kingdoms were motivated by a sense of disgust over clerical ignorance and ecclesiastical corruption. In the case of Scotland, most of the priests and monks were ignorant men, but there were many learned exceptions. Higher clerics were often educated on the Continent, especially at Paris. Schools were few in Scotland during the Middle Ages; about eighteen are known to have been in operation prior to 1284, eight of them monastery schools. In 1496 an act of Parliament required basic education in Latin for sons of nobles and freeholders, but this affected the aristocracy and the gentry only. By the sixteenth century, however, an educational expansion was underway.[26] Three universities had been established in the fifteenth century, and their influence was having significant effects. These institutions were still not renowned, however, and those interested in theology, law, and medicine continued to be attracted to the Continent. The important advances made in education during the fifteenth century did not affect the parish clergy and monks very much, so the Lollard complaints about priests who were unable to instruct congregations were well founded.

The moral condition of the Scottish clergy during the late Middle Ages was, in the eyes of the Lollards, deplorable. A general statute in the thirteenth century had decreed that clerics "shall not in future presume to buy houses or lay properties for the use of concubines and their children. . . . [Priests] must leave nothing by will to their concubines."[27] This law seems to have had little effect on clerical behavior, for in the early sixteenth century Andrew Foreman, archbishop of St. Andrews, found it necessary to issue a synodal constitution forbidding clerics to engage in "unlawful acts." This decree threatened to deprive of their benefices "those who openly keep wenches and concubines, to the grave discredit and injury of the whole church." Foreman specifically commanded offending priests to "put away, eject, and renounce such wenches and concubines, so that . . . no suspicion or

23

scandal can possibly arise." The same order directed priests to devote themselves to serious study and daily attendance at classes held at St. Andrews University.[28] It is ironic, however, that Foreman himself had many secular interests, and his own moral character was blemished.

Ecclesiastical strictures against acquiring properties for the use of concubines reflect the great wealth of the Scottish church in medieval times. By the fifteenth century it was the largest landowner in the kingdom, and nobles often aspired to gain church lands or to dominate appointments to ecclesiastical offices as a means by which to increase their wealth. When bishops made genuine efforts to reform the clergy, they were often hampered because of the ecclesiastical appointments made by the king or powerful aristocratic families.

A major abuse in the Scottish church was the practice of absenteeism. The cathedral chapter at Glasgow, for example, had thirty-two canons in 1455, but only a few actually resided there and rendered services to that church. Although steps were taken to correct this situation, by 1501 the dean of the cathedral and eight canons were still nonresidents.[29] As in England, clerical offices in Scotland were commonly called "livings," and these were often awarded to people without real spiritual interests. Sometimes they went to children too young to understand clerical responsibilities, who were placed in such positions to assure that the income from the benefice would be controlled by the appointee's powerful family. Under such circumstances Patrick Hamilton, who was to become the first martyr of the Scottish Reformation, became titular abbot of Ferne at age thirteen.

Local priests in Scotland, in contrast with the hierarchy, were paid poorly, so they enhanced their incomes by charging fees for various ministries, and they often denied their services to people who could not pay. Episcopal prohibitions of such practices were often ignored, since pastors had no substitute means of income. There was, of course, much resentment toward the clergy because of these financial exactions.[30] There was, in fact, a broad sense of disapproval toward clerics because of their moral and financial irregularities. As one historian observed,

> Poets were not afraid to lampoon the idle monks and friarswits perpetrated jokes at the expense of the voluptuous bishops; and even

24

rustics, when they met at the alehouses told scandalous stories about the parish priest, some concubine he kept, or some good-looking woman he had inveigled at confession.[31]

Since Scottish clergyment were ill-prepared to instruct their parishioners, superstitions were rife in the land. Although he was founder of the University of Aberdeen, and although he tried to reform the clergy of his diocese, Bishop William Elphinstone was a deeply superstitious man himself. In 1507 he published a breviary that was among the first books to be printed in Scotland. (The first vernacular Bible was printed there in 1579.) Elphinstone's breviary contains fabulous miracle tales, such as the story of the lad who accidentally beheaded a robin. When he replaced its head the bird came back to life. Another yarn hails a poor man who killed his only hog to feed St. Serf and his priests. The pig came back to life and reappeared in its pen. St. Serf himself was accredited in the breviary with healing the blind, deaf, and lame, killing a dragon, and raising the dead. Bishop Elphinstone and other leading churchmen accepted such tales at face value.

In Catholic piety the veneration of images as an aid to worship has a long tradition, and in medieval Scotland the practice was customary. As in other countries, this practice became involved in superstitions, which, although not officially endorsed by the church,flourished across the land. It was common for people to recite the *Pater Noster* while kneeling before a statue of the Virgin Mary or one of the saints. The veneration of relics was equally popular. Pope Boniface VIII (1294–1303) claimed that Scotland had been won to Christianity by the relics of St. Andrew, and an arm bone of St. Giles was believed to be in an Edinburgh church.

Scots sometimes went to foreign lands to visit shrines such as the legendary burial place of St. James at Compostella, Spain. Pilgrims from across the seas came to Scotland to pray at so-called holy places, and miracles were said to happen there.[32]

By the opening of the sixteenth century the religious scene in Scotland was closely comparable to that in England. Roman Catholicism was the only officially recognized religion, and, as in practically all of western Europe, church and state were agreed about a policy of resistance to nonconformity. Lollardy had taken root in Scotland, and efforts to destroy it had not succeeded, although the heretics were still only a fractional portion of the

25

population. It is evident, nevertheless, that however small the Lollard movement may have been, it did help to prepare the kingdom for the coming of the Reformation, perhaps because it gained adherents among university students and some of the lower aristocracy. When Lutheranism appeared in Scotland, it found ready acceptance in those areas where Lollardy had taken root earlier.[33]

2

Scotland in the Renaissance

In addition to Lollardy, the spirit of Renaissance humanism helped to prepare the minds of Scotsmen for the Protestant teachings that were brought to Scotland in the early sixteenth century. By that time Renaissance political ideas and the machinery of national monarchy were becoming evident in the northern British kingdom, although the poverty of Scotland did not permit the development of a court and royal administration comparable to that of France, or even England. The Crown relied on middle-class commercial interests for support and maintained generally good relations with the church, despite occasional tensions with the Papacy.

James IV (1488–1513) was a colorful personality who aspired to be a true Renaissance prince and seemed to be committed to good government. His major concerns were to suppress disorderly nobles and to improve the efficiency of his own administration. The highlands were especially unruly, as were some of the off-shore islands.

As evidence of his interest in learning, James IV founded King's College, Aberdeen, and his son founded St. Leonard's College at St. Andrews. In both institutions the spirit of the "new learning," as the humanist method of scholarship was called, was much in evidence. A Royal College of Surgeons opened in 1505, and the printing industry appeared in Scotland in 1507. St. Leonard's College and the printing press were to become key instruments in the eventual success of Protestantism in the kingdom.

Since its relations with England were often hostile, Scotland maintained a traditional political connection with France. When England and France were at war, Scots sometimes invaded England, and, because of the animosity, Scottish graduate students often sought instruction on the Continent rather than at Cambridge or Oxford University.

As early as 1495 some Scots were in contact with Desiderius Erasmus, the great prince of humanists in northern Europe. Hector Boece, a Scottish official at the University of Paris, gave patronage to Erasmus while the latter was a student there at the College of Montaigu, and Boece and other Scots sometimes attended Bible-study sessions that Erasmus conducted. They also met Lefevre d'Etaples (1455–1536), a noteworthy humanists, who, like Erasmus, sought the reform of the Catholic Church through the elimination of corruption and the correction of abuses. Lefevre employed Scotsman David Louis as a proofreader for his textual studies in Greek. Alexander Stewart, archbishop of St. Andrews and son of James IV, obtained instruction in Latin and Greek from Erasmus in 1508, while they were in Siena, and Erasmus was the prelate's traveling companion in Italy as well as his tutor. In addition to these contacts with humanism, it is known that an uncle of King James V was a student of Erasmus, so it appears that a circle of Erasmian-type scholar-reformers had developed at Scotland's royal court by the first decade of the sixteenth century.

There was, of course, some suspicion toward the new learning in Scotland. Bishops and monks who did not seek learning for themselves feared the effect it might have upon others, and some of them charged that the teachings of Erasmus were heretical.

Despite ecclesiastical censures, humanism gained an important following in various parts of Scotland. The influence of Lefevre was strong at the Cistercian abbey at Kinloss. This was due largely to the work of the Italian scholar Giovanni Ferreri, who came into contact with Scots at the University of Paris. One of them, Robert Reid, became abbot of Kinloss and promoted the humane studies for his monks. Eventually that monastery accumulated a large library, and Ferreri gave public lectures on Aristotle and Cicero. Ferreri later supervised the education of James Beaton, who went on to become archbishop of Glasgow. The popularity of studies in classical secular literature did not occlude comparable study of the Bible and ancient Christian sources. Those Scots who became Christian humanists then sought a moral reform of church and society as Erasmus, Lefevre and others were doing on the Continent.[1]

Anglo-Scottish hostility reached something of a climax in 1513, when the forces of Henry VIII dealt a crushing blow to the Scots at the battle of Flodden Field, where James IV and the flower of the Scottish nobility were killed. The death of the king brought his son to the throne as James V (1513–42), and since the new monarch was still a child, his mother served as regent until he reached age sixteen. James V then distinguished himself as a strong ruler and a heroic military leader by suppressing baronial resistance to his authority. He maintained good relations with his Parliament and greatly improved the administration of justice, thereby aiding the growth of royal government.

By the time James V began his personal rule, the Protestant Reformation was underway on the Continent, so the Catholic clerics gave him vigorous support in order to encourage the king to resist Protestant influences. Many Catholic nobles did likewise, and the king responded favorably to his Catholic supporters. In 1538 he married Mary of Guise, a French duchess. In this way James affirmed his Catholic religion and chose to continue the traditional Scottish connection with France at the expense of England.

As the Protestant challenge appeared in Germany and spread across Europe, the Papacy, of course, sought political support wherever it could be found. James V, despite earlier quarrels with Rome, was glad to cooperate with papal designs for the suppression of heresy. In a letter of 31 January 1530 to Pope Clement VII, James declared unswerving loyalty to Roman Catholicism. He took advantage of the pope's dilemma at the same time, however, by asking the pontiff to continue placing in lucrative benefices churchmen who supported royal policies.[2] It seems that for King James, religious duty and political ambition coincided rather nicely.

Henry VIII, after his great victory at Flodden Field, asked the pope to dissolve the archbishopric of St. Andrews and to place Scotland under the jurisdiction of the English Archbishop of York. That would have allowed Henry to make ecclesiastical appointments to positions made vacant by the death of Scottish clerics at Flodden. The pope did not comply and continued formal relations with Scotland, although he did make some clerical appointments without royal consent.[3] It is quite likely that both the Scottish king and the pope were influenced heavily by Renaissance political pragmatism. Although both opposed religious non-conformity and agreed to work to suppress it, they did not pursue the internal reform of the church that was needed so badly in Christendom at large and in Scotland in particular. Without a papal, episcopal, and royal commitment, such a reform was practically impossible.

Although Renaissance humanism exerted considerable influence upon Scotland, and its kings and churchmen sometimes behaved like Renaissance princes, Catholicism of a medieval character remained strong in the land. The career of John Major (1469–1550) illustrates this well.

Major was a distinguished scholar and teacher who studied at Cambridge University before moving to Paris in 1493, where he received the master of arts degree in 1496. He became a professor of arts and Scholastic philosophy at the College of Montaigu in Paris and lectured at the College of Navarre there as well. In 1505 Major was awarded the doctor of divinity degree, and about that time he joined the faculty of theology at the Sorbonne.

John Major was a prolific author of philosophical, historical, and theological treatises. He wrote expositions of Aristotle's logic and that great thinker's *Ethics,* and he composed commentaries on the *Four Books of Sentences* by Peter Lombard, which was the principal textbook for the teaching of theology until the Reformation. In biblical studies this learned Scot produced commentaries on the Gospels. His chief contribution as a historian is a work entitled *Historia Majoris Britanniae,* which he finished in 1520.[4] By that time he had returned to Scotland, where his reputation had preceded him. Some of the students he had taught in Paris went on to become noteworthy scholars and authors themselves.

Upon returning to his native land, Major joined the faculty at the University of Glasgow, which had been until that time a rather undistinguished institution. His presence on the faculty of arts, however, made the university attractive, and a large increase in enrollment occurred. In 1522 Major moved to St. Andrews University, where he remained until 1526, when he returned to Paris. Patrick Hamilton, who was to become Scotland's first Protestant martyr, studied under Major at St. Andrews, as did George Buchanan, who later became a historian of note and a champion of the Protestant cause.

During his two terms in Paris, John Major became acquainted

with Christian humanism. He was at the university there at the same time as Erasmus (ca. 1499), and during his second stay (1526–31), John Calvin, Ignatius Loyola, Reginald Pole, François Rabelais, and other distinguished advocates of the new learning were there. Despite the growing influence of humanism in the French capital, however, Major remained an adherent to medieval Scholasticism, as his commentary on the Gospels indicates.[5] He was resolute in his opposition to heresy, and he seems to have endorsed the use of force to combat it. This is evident in his writing about the reign of the English king Henry V (1413–22), where he reported with approval the burning of some Lollards "who spoke wicked things of [against] the church and the clergy."[6]

By 1526, when Major was in Paris, the Lutheran controversy was raging on the Continent and had begun to infiltrate the British Isles. Erasmus was suspected of being a crypto-Lutheran, and Major joined in the criticism against him. For the Lutherans he had nothing but scorn. This may have been related closely to their rejection of transubstantation, because the belief that the bread and wine of the Eucharist become the actual body and blood of Christ was one that Major cherished and defended vigorously. In his commentary on the Gospel of Matthew he was especially aggressive in denoucning Wycliffe, Luther, Zwingli, and any others who denied transubstantiation.[7]

Although he was suspicious of humanism and belligerent toward Protestantism, Major admitted that some of the criticisms of the Catholic Church made by these men were well founded. Like Erasmus and Luther, he denounced the sale of indulgences, but he upheld clerical celibacy, monasticism, the veneration of the saints, and the use of images in Christian worship. In the words of one biographer, Major stood "in the old paths of the Roman and Catholic Church and treat[ed] all deviations from its doctrine as pestilent and poisonous heresy. But like the best Romanists of his age, he favour[ed] reforms within the church and by the church itself."[8]

Christian humanists, both Catholic and Protestant, found John Major's defense of the old order very irritating. Philip Melanchthon, Luther's co-worker at the University of Wittenberg, in defending Luther against the theologians of the Sorbonne, assailed Major as an opponent of the truth, and the scholar-rationalist Rabelais employed biting satire to ridicule Major. In the *Inestima-*

ble Life of the Great Gargantua, Father of Pantagruel, Rabelais put into the mouth of Pantagruel the taunt that Major had written an absurd treatise entitled *The Art of Making Puddings.*[9]

John Major, it is clear, was not an obscurantist. His historical writings are much superior to those of the medieval chroniclers, and he was not indifferent to the problems of ignorance and corruption in his church, which he desired to reform. For him, however, the body of traditional doctrine was sacrosanct and therefore not open to revision. He represented the best in Scholastic learning at that time, and it must have grieved him deeply to see that some of those who studied under him—for example, Patrick Hamilton and George Buchanan—abandoned Catholicism and embraced the Protestant faith.

Because of his stature within the Roman Catholic Church, when Major admitted the legitimacy of many humanist and Protestant charges, he may have unwittingly aided the eventual triumph of the heresy that he despised. Catholic Scotland remained resistant to reform, even to that of the moderate character proposed by Erasmus, Lefevre, and other devout Catholic scholars. By his determined defense of medieval doctrines and ecclesiastical practices, Major and those who shared his views helped to discourage the Scottish Church from initiating changes that might have made the Protestant cause less appealing to their countrymen. While Renaissance humanism exerted considerable influence upon the political life of Scotland, its effects on the church were relatively slight. When religious reform came to Scotland, therefore, it was the work of Protestants, initially the work of Martin Luther's disciples.

3

The Rise of Scottish Protestantism

When the Protestant faith arrived in Scotland its harbinger was probably not a Scot but a Frenchman—M. de la Tour—who went there in 1523 to work in the employ of the duke of Albany. De la Tour appears to have been the first link in the chain of transmission that brought Luther's teachings to Scotland, although numerous Scots went to the Continent to study, and about sixty of them were at the University of Paris by 1500. Since Lutheran ideas became current in Paris by 1519, some Scots must have become acquainted with them. M. de la Tour, after he returned to France, was accused of spreading Lutheran heresy in Scotland. He was executed on orders of the *Parlement* of Paris in 1527, on that specific charge. Unfortunately, very little is known about him, so there is no way to measure the degree of his influence in bringing the Protestant faith to the land in which he was employed.

Whatever the role of de la Tour may have been, it is evident that the coming of the English-language New Testament to Scotland was a factor of monumental importance in the Reformation there. This occurred at the very time that Thomas Cardinal Wolsey, chief minister to Henry VIII, was trying to prevent the importation and distribution of the New Testament in England. Early in 1526 John Hackett, English ambassador in Antwerp, wrote to Wolsey that there were "divers merchants of Scotland that bought many such like books and took them into Scotland, a part to Edinburgh, and most to the town of St. Andrews."[1] Several Scottish ports traded with Zealand, so there were ample opportunities to smuggle Bibles and unapproved religious literature into the kingdom. The Scottish Parliament had enacted a law in 1525 to prohibit importation of Luther's books, and an act of 1527 extended the penalties to Scots who abetted such importation. These decrees may have been issued in reaction to the teaching of Patrick Hamilton, which had already aroused the opposition of Catholic authorities.[2] Protestant books from England began appearing in Scotland about the same time that William Tyndale's English translation of the New Testament made its debut there.

Concurrent with the arrival of Tyndale's New Testament and some Lutheran literature, Sir David Lyndsay published material that was highly critical of ecclesiastical corruption. Lyndsay's early poems seem to show the influence of Lollard ideas. His *Testament and Complaynt of the Papyngo* is of this character,[3] and *The Dreme of Sir David Lyndsay,* which was published about 1528, is a biting attack upon corruption from the pen of a Catholic who enjoyed the royal favor. In this "dream" the author saw a vision of hell, where the most prominent residents were "proud, perverse, prelates, innumerable priors, abbots, and false, flattering friars groaning in agony."[4] Lyndsay related that the clerics in hell were suffering the just consequences of their greed and lust. In his judgment Scotland's churchmen had debased the kingdom and had thereby brought it under the judgment of God.

Although he exposed the condition of the church in Scotland and indicted those whom he held responsible for it, Lyndsay did not call for a religious revolution. His perspective on the matter was that of a reformer who pleaded for a moral and administrative cleansing of church and society, a plea that he made even more vivid later in *A Satire of the Three Estates* (1540), where he called on King James V to lead a reformation of abuses.[5] Because of his friendship with the king, Lyndsay was not molested by the Catholic hierarchy, which found his writings, to say the least, irritating and embarrassing. The publications of this critic show that little had been done to eliminate corruption from the Scottish church since the fourteenth century, when the Lollards had raised essentially the same complaints. By the sixteenth century Scots had grown accustomed to exposés of clerical abuses, and neither lords nor commoners were uncritical in their loyalty to the Roman Catholic church.[6]

The lamentations of David Lyndsay, presented with artistic skill, helped to focus attention on the deplorable state of religion in Scotland, and the author thereby helped to prepare the country for the coming of the Protestant Reformation. The Catholic hierarchy, on the other hand, contributed unwittingly to the success of Protestanism by its stubborn refusal to initiate needed changes.[7]

Due to the decadent condition of Scottish Catholicism and the resistance of its leaders to reform, the stage was set for the appearance of Patrick Hamilton, who became Luther's Scottish disciple. Neither the exact date nor place of his birth has been ascertained, but the evidence at hand suggests he was born about 1503, probably at Stanehouse, Lanarkshire, although it may have been at Kincavel, Linlithgow. His death occurred at the hands of his enemies at St. Andrews on 29 February 1528, when he was barely twenty-five years old. Scotland's first Protestant martyr was a son of Sir Patrick Hamilton and Catherine Stewart, a daughter of the duke of Albany. The Hamiltons were descended from the Anglo-Normans and traced their ancestry to Robert, first earl of Leicester, who had accompanied William the Conqueror to England in 1066. On both his father's and his mother's side, Patrick Hamilton was related to Scotland's royal family. Peter Lorimer, the only real biographer of Scotland's first native Lutheran, described his subject's heritage in these glowing terms:

> With the best blood of Scotland in his veins, and with the most heroic and accomplished men of the kingdom to form the mind and manners of his early age, it was only natural that he should grow up to be what he afterwards became; when the endeavors of divine grace had been added to the gifts of nature and the accomplishments of education—not only the most zealous, but the most courteous evangelist—a confessor of the truth, . . . a martyr as learned and cultured as he was fervent, . . . a master of all the new learning of his age, as well instinct with all its revived religious zeal and ardour.[8]

Although Lorimer may have been a bit too profuse in estimating the abilities of Patrick Hamilton, the records show clearly that his subject was a man of deep religious piety, theological learning, and conspicuous courage.

Because of his family's social standing and political influence, Patrick Hamilton was placed in a lucrative ecclesiastical benefice at an early age, when he was made titular abbot of Ferne in 1517. Such benefices were objects of great aristocratic greed, competed for by the most powerful families of the realm. In some cases barons did not wait for vacanices to occur in church offices; they simply created them by murder or seized them in petty civil wars.

The practice of placing sons of aristocrats in church offices *in commendam*, meant that their families could enjoy the revenues of the benefice while the responsibilities of the office were delegated to someone other than the son who bore the title. Commendam took the election of monastic abbots and priors away from the monks. Under this arrangement children such as Patrick Hamilton did not actually become monks or priests, did not reside in a monastery, and did not wear monastic garb. By the time young Hamilton received the office at Ferne, a Premonstratensian abbey in Rosshire, the entitlement of absentee churchmen had become a long-standing abuse in Scottish Catholicism. Not only monastic officials but the so-called secular clerics had been engaging in such practices for a long time. Secular bishops often lived in France or Italy and left their episcopal duties to subordinates at home.[9]

With the substantial income from his benefice to support him, Patrick Hamilton went to the University of Paris from which he received a master of arts degree in 1520. It is not clear whether he studied in one or two colleges at Paris. The College of Grisy was known as the Scots' college. It had been founded by David Murray, Bishop of Moray, during the reign of King Robert I, the Bruce (1274–1329) and, being a Scotsman, Hamilton might naturally have enrolled there. The other possibility (the more probable one) was the College of Montaigu, which had become well known to Scottish students through the renowned teaching of John Major.

While at Paris, Hamilton became acquainted with two intellectual/religious movements that led him to develop a strong disdain for the Scholastic philosophy/theology that dominated the teaching there. These movements were Catholic humanism, as promoted by Erasmus and his followers, and Protestant theology, as proclaimed by Luther and the German reformers. His attraction to Erasmian concepts must have been especially strong at that point, because he moved to the University of Louvain in the Low Countries soon after receiving his degree. Erasmus had preceded him to Louvain and had been teaching there since 1517. The pioneer English Lutheran reformer Robert Barnes was there at the same time.[10]

Patrick Hamilton appears to have distinguished himself as a scholar in classical languages and Platonic philosophy at Louvain, and his mastery of those languages would have allowed him to use the New Testament in Greek and Latin that Erasmus had published as the first critically prepared edition of the Christian scriptures.

Although by the time he went to Louvain Patrick Hamilton had no affinity for medieval Scholasticism, he may have been drawn to the Augustinian friars at Antwerp, who were very receptive to the new learning. Some of them later became martyrs for the Protestant faith.[11] Robert Barnes, for example, was an Augustian prior who brought classical learning from the Low Countries to his fellow monks at Cambridge.[12]

While Hamilton was still in Paris, the university there became agitated by the circulation of Lutheran ideas that Catholic theologians regarded as the consequence of Erasmian teaching. Martin Luther reported in a letter to Johann Lange in April 1519 that his writings were being read and discussed at the Sorbonne.[13] The next year university officials ordered the burning of Luther's works, a decree that, of course, aroused great interest in the teachings of the German reformer and helped thereby to disseminate his ideas widely. Since Patrick Hamilton was at the University of Paris while the Lutheran matter was being debated, he must have acquired some knowledge of the controversial doctrines coming from Germany. There is no evidence, however, that he embraced Lutheranism at that time. Like his English contemporaries Robert Barnes and William Tyndale, Hamilton's passage from medieval Catholicism to evangelical Protestantism was via Erasmian humanism. He became a moral reformer and critic of ignorance and corruption at first and moved from that posture finally into the role of a theological reformer.

Unfortunately, the evidence available does not permit a definitive judgment on the question of exactly how much influence Erasmus exerted on Hamilton, but the young Scot returned to his homeland in 1523 and joined the Faculty of Arts at St. Andrews University at the same time that the eminent John Major went there at the urging of James Beaton, archbishop of St. Andrews. The records state that Hamilton was "incorporated" into the university in June 1523, which appears to mean that he became a postgraduate student and an instructor of undergraduates.[14] By that time St. Leonard's College enjoyed the services of John Major; George Buchanan, who, like Patrick Hamilton, became a leading Protestant reformer, was a student there, as were Alexander Alesius and John Wedderburn, who also became leading Protestants. Major may have encouraged these men to seek the moral reform of the church.[15]

When Patrick Hamilton joined the faculty of arts at St. Andrews University in 1523, it had become the foremost institution of higher learning in the kingdom. Humanism, however, had not yet achieved a pronounced influence there. The legislation that established St. Leonard's College in 1512 showed no trace of the humanist spirit. The church both encouraged and discouraged the new learning. Some prominent clerics subsidized humane studies and participated in them themselves. Monks, friars, and the lower clergy, for the most part, opposed such pursuits.[16]

Although he was reasonably well informed about Luther's doctrine when he began teaching at St. Andrews, Patrick Hamilton did not assail Catholic dogma at that time. He instead attacked entrenched moral evils and abusive ecclesiastical practices. This was, of course, not heresy, but those who were threatened by such indictments often accused those who exposed them of heresy. Hamilton therefore was engaging in a rather dangerous cause. His principal criticism at first was concerned with traditional educational policies at the university. He called in particular for implementation of the humanist methodology, which entailed the study of primary documents rather than secondary interpretations alone. He challenged the Scholastics, for example, to reconsider Aristotle in this manner. During this period Hamilton composed choral music for masses, which is further evidence that this critic of ignorance had not yet become a heretic.[17]

Whether Patrick Hamilton was ordained to the priesthood during his stay in St. Andrews (1523–26) is difficult to determine. John Frith (1503–33), the English reformer who was responsible for printing Hamilton's only theological writing, stated that the Scot "took upon him priesthood," and Lorimer and some more recent interpreters have accepted Frith's statement at face value.[18] Others have contended that Frith must have been mistaken, because Hamilton was not degraded from the priesthood at the time of his trial and execution, and his accusers would not have missed an opportunity to humiliate him in that way.[19] In the text of the charges brought against him there is no mention of his violating the priestly vow of celibacy.[20]

The question about Patrick Hamilton's clerical status or the lack thereof involves more than satisfying academic curiosity about an obscure aspect in the life of a rather remote figure. Shortly before he was killed by Catholic authorities, Hamilton had married a lady of aristocratic rank whose name has not been preserved, and he sired a daughter, who was born after her father's death. Had he been a priest, it is highly probable that his marriage would have been used against him at this trial. Surely, some mention of it would have appeared in the indictment. The three records that document the charges, however, contain no reference to a marriage.[21] Patrick Hamilton may have been in minor orders, but it seems quite unlikely that he was a priest.

While the question of Hamilton's clerical standing will probably never be resolved, his criticisms of the Scottish clergy were bound to provoke opposition. Defenders of traditional methods in teaching and study at the university found his fervent advocacy of the new learning objectionable, and they reacted as threatened vested interests usually do. Since Lutheran teachings were being denounced as heresy throughout the Roman Catholic church, it was easy to embarrass or silence an annoying critic of church or schools by calling him a Lutheran. By 1526 this device was being used with considerable success against Hamilton, and, since he would not be silent, the tempo of accusations increased steadily. Although he was probably not yet a convinced Lutheran, he had begun to show sympathy for some of the German reformer's positions. Hamilton may have been regarded as an especially serious menace to the Catholic church in Scotland because he was of royal blood and had many influential relatives.

The situation in his homeland became very dangerous for Patrick Hamilton when his conduct was brought to the attention of Archbishop James Beaton. This distinguished prelate was representative of the kind of churchman both Catholic and Protestant reformers cited in their criticisms. Beaton (d. 1539) was educated at St. Andrews University, from which he received a master of arts degree in 1493. He became archbishop of Glasgow in 1509, and he moved to the diocese of St. Andrews in 1522. As archbishop there he was primate over the Catholic church in Scotland. He was also lord treasurer and lord chancellor of the kingdom of Scotland for several years. During the minority of King James V, Beaton sat on a commission of regency, where he exerted substantial influence over affairs of state.

As a churchman Beaton was a practitioner of pluralism, a corrupt custom that allowed a person to hold several benefices and receive their lucrative revenues concurrently. He was prior to the monastery at Whithorn and abbot at Dunfermline, Kilwinning, and Arbroath. When he became Archbishop of St. Andrews, he bequeathed the abbacy of Arbroath to his nephew David Beaton but reserved the income from it for himself. When the Hamilton and Douglas factions fought for power during the minority of James V, Archbishop Beaton participated in the armed combat and almost lost his life. Once in the position of primate at St. Andrews, he quarreled bitterly with his successor at Glasgow, and those conflicts led occasionally to actual violence and frantic appeals to Rome. John Knox summarized the Protestant attitude toward this prelate crisply:

> James Beaton, son of the Laird of Balfour in Fife, who was more careful for the world than he was to preach Christ, or yet to advance any religion but for the fashion only; and as he sought the world, it fled [from] him not, for it was well known that he at once was Archbishop of St. Andrews, abbot of Dunfermline, Arbroath, Kilwinning, and chancellor of Scotland. . . . [He suppressed God's truth] till it pleased God of his great mercy . . . to raise up his servant *Master Patrick Hamilton,* at whom our history doth begin.[22]

Once he was convinced that the archbishop meant to apprehend him, Patrick Hamilton took the advice of friends who urged him to flee from the country. He arrived in Wittenberg, Germany, in May 1527, where he seems to have stayed only a brief time, and little is known about his exact relationship with Luther, Melanchthon, and other theologians at the university there. From the character of his doctrine developed on the Continent and proclaimed soon after in Scotland, however, it is evident that Hamilton became a convinced Lutheran during his sojourn in Germany. It seems that he did not enroll formally in classes at Wittenberg, but he was in a position to listen to theological lectures, to attend preaching services, and to discourse with scholars and students who promulgated the Lutheran faith. Lorimer speculated that Patrick Hamilton may have left Wittenberg hurriedly to avoid contagion from bubonic plague, which afflicted the town at that time.[23]

Whatever his reason for doing so, Hamilton left Wittenberg for Marburg, where Philip, prince of Hesse, had just founded a Protestant university, the first in Europe to be established without the approval of the Papacy.[24] Philip, who had become one of the leading Protestant princes in Germany, invited some highly distinguished scholars to his university. Johannes Ferrarius Montanus became professor of civil law and rector of the institution, while Johannes Feige, chief judge of Hesse, became its chancellor. The most important member of the faculty in terms of his relationship with Patrick Hamilton was Francis Lambert of Avignon, professor of theology, a reformer who, like Hamilton, has not received attention commensurate with his contributions to the Protestant cause.[25]

Lambert had joined the Observant Franciscans as a boy of fifteen, but his experience among the friars left him dismayed by their lack of genuine piety, despite their formal commitment to abide strictly by the rule of St. Francis. Lambert's evident intelligence and devotion to monastic duty led his superiors to make him a preacher, an action that aroused jealousy among other friars. Despite such envy, he was promoted after several years to the position of "apostolic preacher" of the Order of Friars Minor. This required Lambert to travel widely as a public herald seeking the salvation of souls, a task he performed with conspicuous zeal. In order to prepare for his preaching, he gave great attention to Bible study, and he consequently became a popular expositor of Scripture and an exhorter calling people to God.

In addition to the jealousy of other friars, Francis Lambert incurred charges of heresy when it appeared that he was espousing ideas suspiciously similar to the teachings of Martin Luther. In fact, he had been reading Luther's treatises for sometime, and that experience aroused within him a desire to meet the reformer of Wittenberg in person in order to discuss the points at issue between him and Rome. This desire led Lambert eventually to leave the Franciscans.

Before he was able to establish contact with Luther, Lambert went to Zurich, where he met Ulrich Zwingli, leader of the reform in that part of German Switzerland. During discussions between these theologians Lambert tried to defend some traditional Catholic doctrines such as the intercessory work of the Virgin Mary and other saints. Zwingli, however, rebutted his arguments effectively, and Lambert then renounced Roman Catholicism in 1522. The next year he entered the University of Wittenberg to study the Bible, and soon thereafter he married.

Philip Melanchthon, Luther's closest friend and co-worker, was so impressed with Lambert's learning and piety that he recommended him to Philip of Hesse, who appointed him to the theological faculty at Marburg, an institution that held classes in buildings confiscated by the prince from Catholic monks. One hundred and five students and professors composed the academic community when the university opened in 1527. Patrick Hamilton was there for the occasion.

When Francis Lambert first went to Marburg, he must have been a convinced Lutheran, or Melanchthon would not have recommended him for a faculty position. There is decisive evidence to show that Lambert held Luther's position on sin and salvation, for he wrote *De Arbitrio Hominis vere Captivo,* which espouses the view of human depravity that Luther set forth boldly in *De Servo Arbitrio* (1525), his reply to an attack from Erasmus.

Lambert, in the early years of his career as a Protestant reformer, endorsed Luther's teaching on the Eucharist that the body and blood of Christ are truly present in, with, and under the bread and wine, though the elements are not changed (transubstantiated), as in the Roman Catholic teaching. After spending some time in Strassburg, where he was exposed to the interpretation that the Eucharist is entirely symbolic, he abandoned Luther's doctrine for that of Zwingli. A careful study of Lambert's mature thinking shows that he was a composite figure in whom concepts from Franciscan legalism were blended with others from the teachings of Luther, Zwingli, and Martin Bucer, the reformer of Strassburg.[26]

The degree of Francis Lambert's influence on Patrick Hamilton is difficult to assess, but it is clear that the two were together at that period in Lambert's life when he still espoused the Lutheran confession, so it appears that he encouraged Hamilton to continue in the Lutheran persuasion to which he had already given allegiance.

Lambert appreciated Hamilton's devotion to the reform and encouraged his scholarly endeavors at Marburg. As a consequence the young Scotsman composed *Dyvers Frutful Gatherings of Scripture Concernyng Fayth and Workes,* a doctrinal treatise written first in Latin and translated into English about 1532 by John Frith, who, along with William Tyndale, was at Marburg when Patrick Hamilton did his writing. The treatise soon became known as *Patrick's Places,* the first theological writing of the Protestant Reformation in Scotland. Frith, the translator, called this document "the pith of all divinity."[27]

Patrick's Places is a doctrinal treatise on salvation arranged in accordance with Luther's teaching regarding the relationship of law and gospel as the means of revelation about man's sin and his hope for deliverance from it. This is not merely a protest against moral and administrative abuses in the church, which a Catholic humanist would have written. The work is decidedly theological in character and emphasizes justification *sola fide,* the keystone of the Reformation. One recent historian said *Patrick's Places* "contain[s] the pure milk of the Lutheran word."[28] Hamilton and his fellow reformers would have preferred to regard it as containing the pure milk of the Word of God. Since the text of Hamilton's composition is brief and merits reading in full, it has been included as an appendix to this book.

Patrick's Places, although its content would be acceptable to both the Lutheran and the Reformed branches of Protestantism, reflects primarily (but not exclusively) the influence of Martin Luther, particularly his treatise *The Freedom of a Christian,* which he published in 1520. It also appears to mirror the influence of Melanchthon's systematic theology in *Locis Communes* (1521) and Tyndale's *The Parable of the Wicked Mammon* (1527).[29] Hamilton's work lists eight propositions that pertain to the law of God and ten that pertain to the gospel of Christ.

In arranging his treatise in terms of the law/gospel motif, Hamilton was employing the interpretive method that Luther believed is indispensable for a correct understanding of Scripture. For Luther, Christ is the heart and center of the entire Bible, the living Word of God, who conveys pardon for sin through the gospel. The Bible is God's Word, the means by which he speaks to mankind through law and gospel, which are two channels of special revelation. Luther explained his teaching on this matter in his 1535 commentary on St. Paul's letter to the Galatians.

> It is sufficiently evident what the distinction is between the Law and the Gospel. The Law never brings the Holy Spirit; therefore it does not justify, because it only teaches what we ought to do. But the Gospel does bring the Holy Spirit, because it teaches what we ought to receive. Therefore the Law and the Gospel are two altogether contrary doctrines. Accordingly, to put righteousness into the Law is simply to conflict with the Gospel. For the Law is a taskmaster; it demands that

43

we work and that we give. In short, it wants to have something from us. The Gospel, on the contrary, does not demand; it grants freely; it commands us to hold out our hands and to receive what is being offered. Now demanding and granting are exact opposites and cannot exist together. . . . Therefore, if the Gospel is a gift and offers a gift, it does not demand anything. On the other hand, the Law does not grant anything; it makes demands on us, and impossible ones at that.[30]

Luther believed that law and gospel run parallel throughout both the Old Testament and the New Testament. Both of the major divisions of the Bible contain demands for human works in terms of the law, and both proclaim free pardon for sin, which is the heart of the gospel. The law exposes man's sin and declares him guilty and condemned before his holy God. The gospel reveals the work of Christ, who suffered as a substitute for sinners by taking the penalty prescribed by the law upon himself. He therefore satisfied divine justice, and he imparts forgiveness to sinners who repent and receive him through faith.

Patrick Hamilton began his dissertation by citing the Ten Commandments. He then drew his readers' attention to the summary of those precepts given by Christ.

All these commandments are briefly comprised in these two. . . ; "Love the Lord your God with all your heart, with all your soul, and with all your mind. This is the first and great commandment. The second is like unto this. That is, love your neighbor as yourself. On these two commandments hang all the law and the prophets" (Matthew 22:37–40).[31]

Through a series of logical syllogisms, Hamilton expounded his belief that love for God is the basis for keeping the divine commandments. He argued that perfect love for God would produce perfect love for one's neighbors, and such love would demonstrate itself by perfect obedience to God's laws. Hamilton's method of argumentation was as follows:

First Proposition: He that loves God loves his neighbor.

Second Proposition: He that loves his neighbor as himself keeps all the commandments of God.

44

Argument:
  Major
  Premise: He that loves his neighbor keeps all the command-
        ments of God.
  Minor
  Premise: He that loves God loves his neighbor.

Conclusion: He that loves God keeps all the commandments of
        God.

Third Proposition: He that has faith loves God.

Argument:
  Major
  Premise: He that keeps the commandments of God has the
        love of God.
  Minor
  Premise: He that has faith keeps the commandments of God.

Conclusion: He that has faith loves God.[32]

In each syllogism Hamilton buttressed his argument with cita-
tions from Scripture, which for him was the final authority to
which all his reasoning was subject.

After explaining the indispensability of love and faith before
one can obey the law, Hamilton contended that since it is impossible to keep any of the commandments of God without grace, and
it is not in our power to have grace, it is therefore not in our
power to keep any of the commandments of God. He attributed
the ability to live by the divine precepts to the ministry of the Holy
Spirit, who grants faith to believe the Word of God. "Concerning
the Holy Spirit and faith, . . . without them we are unable to keep
any of the commandments of God."[33]

Hamilton asserted that while the law is a perfect standard for
human behavior, "the keeping of the commandments is to us
impossible. . . . The law commands us to do what is impossible."
He rebutted the objection that God would not expect man to do
the impossible by arguing that the divine law has another purpose, which is

to make you know that you are but evil, and that there is no remedy to save you in your own hand [ability]: and that you may seek remedy at [from] some other, for the law does nothing else but command you.[34]

After relating the biblical teaching on the human dilemma caused by sin, the young Scottish theologian proceeded to explain the divine remedy, which is the essence of the gospel. He did so at first by contrasting the nature and function of the law and the gospel.

The law shows us our sin (Romans 3). The gospel shows us remedy for it (John 1). The law shows us our condemnation (Romans 7). The gospel shows us our redemption (Colossians 1). The law is the word of ire (Romans 4). The gospel is the word of grace (Acts 20). The law is the word of despair (Deuteronomy 27). The gospel is the word of comfort (Luke 2). The law is the word of unrest (Romans 7). The gospel is the word of peace (Ephesians 6).

In *Patrick's Places* the above is followed by

"A Disputation between the Law and the Gospel. . . .

The law says, "pay your debt." The gospel says, "Christ has paid it." The law says, "you are a sinner; despair and you shall be damned." The gospel says, "you are forigven; be of good comfort; you shall be saved." The law says, "make amends for your sins." The gospel says, "Christ has made it for you." The law says, "the Father in heaven is angry with you." The gospel says, "Christ has pacified him with his blood." The law says, "where is your righteousness, your goodness, your satisfaction?" The gospel says, "Christ is your righteousness, your goodness, your satisfaction." The law says, "you are bound and obliged to me, to the devil, and to hell." The gospel says, "Christ has delivered you from them all."[35]

This rather elaborate and somewhat repetitious argument is actually a preface to lead readers to consider the doctrine of justification through faith alone, which is the grand theme of *Patrick's Places*. Hamilton defined saving faith as a gift from God that enables a person to believe and trust in Christ. Man cannot produce faith; it is not a natural faculty that man may employ at will.

Faith is to believe God, as Abraham believed God and it was imputed to him for righteousness. To believe God is to believe his Word, and to account it true what he says. He that does not believe God's word does not believe God himself. He that does not believe God's Word regards him false and a liar and does not believe that he will fulfill his Word; and so he denies both the might of God and God himself.[36]

He that has faith believes God. He that believes God believes his Word. He that believes his Word knows well that he is true and faithful and may not lie, knowing that he . . . will fulfill his Word.[37]

Hamilton held that saving faith brings assurance that one's sins have been forgiven because Christ died in his place. This faith is not merely an affirmation of traditional religious dogmas. It is a personal trust in Christ alone for salvation. Those who possess such faith actually know God and are justified through faith as they stand before him. "Faith alone makes a man good and righteous. . . . Faith extols God and his deeds."[38]

Because Hamilton, like Luther, proclaimed the doctrine of salvation by grace alone, he scorned the medieval teaching that somehow human works contribute toward securing the favor of God. The young Scottish reformer declared,

Whosoever believes or thinks to be saved by his works denies that Christ is his savior, that Christ died for him, and that all things pertain to Christ. For how is he your savior, if you might save yourself by your works, or whereto should he die for you, if any works might have saved you?[39]

Patrick Hamilton believed that placing confidence in one's works is the equivalent of claiming that one is his own Christ.

Hamilton's argument assumed the validity of the Pauline/Augustinian doctrine of predestination. He admonished Christians to be grateful "for the love he [God] had for you before you were born, when you had done neither good nor evil."[40] This was practically a universal belief among sixteenth-century Protestants, beginning with Luther, whose major treatise on salvation, *The Bondage of the Will* (1525), became the classic of Reformation writing on predestination.[41]

Hamilton argued vigorously that salvation is monergistic, that is, it is the work of God alone, not a synergistic matter of divine/human cooperation. This was a hallmark of Protestant teaching, which Luther expressed succinctly in his Small Catechism:

I believe that I cannot by my own reason or strength believe in Jesus Christ, my Lord, or come to him; but his Holy Spirit has called me through the gospel, enlightened me by his gifts and sanctified and preserved me in the true faith.[42]

Luther, Hamilton, and others who proclaimed salvation *sola gratia* and justification *sola fide* often encountered the criticism that their teaching disparaged good works and thereby promoted an attitude of indifference toward Christian moral responsibilities. Luther responded to this charge in a number of his writings. In his *Theses Concerning Faith and Law* (1535) he wrote. "[G]ood works must follow faith, yes, not only must, but follow voluntarily, just as a good tree not only must produce good fruits, but does so freely."[43]

Patrick Hamilton, like Martin Luther, denied forcefully that his teaching on justification encouraged moral laxity and indifference toward good works.[44] After asserting, "we should do no good works to the intent of getting the inheritance of heaven or remission of sin," he explained,

> I do not condemn good deeds, but I condemn the false trust in any works; for all the works in which man puts any confidence are therewith poisoned and become evil. Therefore, you must do good works, but be aware [that] you do not do them to deserve any good through them; for if you do receive the good not as the gifts of God but as a debt to you, you make yourself fellow with God, because you will accept nothing from him for nothing.[45]

Patrick Hamilton's beliefs, like those of his English contemporaries William Tyndale and Robert Barnes, have been subjected to revisionist interpretations.[46] In an article in the *Archive For Reformation History*, Iain R. Torrance contends that Hamilton taught the Scholastic doctrine of "infused grace." That is, God gives man power to perform works of merit that enable him to acquire a personal righteousness, which in turn qualifies him for acceptance by his maker. Torrance understands Hamilton to have taught that Christ "bought us from the guilt of our individual sins but did not redeem our corrupted nature."[47] Torrance argues that Hamilton did not hold to the forensic concept of redemption that was at the heart of Luther's theology. The conclusions that Torrance advances are conspicuously lacking in evidential support, either from the writings of Hamilton himself or from those of his contemporaries. It is clear that his Roman Catholic accusers did not believe that Hamilton's soteriology was compatible with the Scholastic teachings of the late Middle Ages.

It appears that Patrick Hamilton remained in Germany only about six months. He returned to Scotland late in 1527, and at first Catholic authorities allowed him considerable freedom to preach the evangelical message. It is possible that they did so in order to allow him to incriminate himself thoroughly by the proclamation of heresy. Since he belonged to the powerful family of Hamilton, his enemies had to be sure that their case against him would be indisputable. In the words of Lorimer, "A Lutheran missionary with royal blood in his veins and all the power of the Hamiltons at his back was a more formidable heretic in Scotland than Luther himself would have been."[48]

Either because he was ignorant of their designs, or because he was heedless of the danger involved, the young missionary played right into the hands of his enemies. For about a month he preached and taught in St. Andrews University, where he exerted great influence upon students, faculty members, and various orders of clerics and monks.

James Beaton, archbishop of St. Andrews, assumed direction of the effort to silence Hamilton, and at first it seems that Beaton wanted to accomplish that end without executing him. If the troublesome preacher had been driven into exile, Beaton would not have run so great a risk in antagonizing the reformer's potent family and friends. In pursuit of this design the prelate lured Hamilton with an offer to discuss some ecclesiastical practices that might be reformed. Some of his friends detected a plot and urged Patrick to flee, but he refused to leave Scotland. He was duly apprehended once Beaton was satisfied that the evidence against him was sufficient to secure a condemnation.

The trial of Patrick Hamilton took place before a council composed of bishops, abbots, priors, theologians, and Black and Grey Friars. A friar named Alexander Campbell read the indictment, which accused Hamilton of heresy. Robert Lindesay of Piscottie, a Protestant historian of the sixteenth century, related that Hamilton asserted to his captors that people have the right and the duty to read the Word of God, especially the New Testament, in order to "know their own sins and [to] repent for the same, whereby they may amend their lives by faith and repentance and come to the mercy of God by Christ Jesus."[49]

During the interrogation Hamilton decried the idolatrous use of images in the church by quoting the Second Commandment and by contending that King David in the Psalms "curses those who make images . . . and [the] worshippers of the same." When his accuser objected that images are necessary for "the common people, to put them in remembrance of holy saints who wrait [wrought] for their salvation," Hamilton replied, "Brother, it ought to be the preaching of the true Word of God that should put the people in remembrance of Christ and their salvation."[50] In this way the accused heretic denied the mediatorship of the Virgin Mary and departed saints. He quoted the words of St. Paul, "There is one God and one mediator between God and man, the man Christ Jesus" (1 Tim. 2:5), and he contended that those who pray to saints thereby reject the mediatorial office of Christ.[51] When Campbell and other friars implored him to recant and to call on the Virgin Mary, Hamilton retorted, "Depart and trouble me not, you messengers of Satan."[52]

Another point on which Hamilton rejected traditional Catholic teaching was the matter of purgatory. He said that he found no such place mentioned in Scripture. He affirmed, on the contrary, that he believed "there is one thing that may purge the soul of man,. . . the blood of Jesus Christ," and he called his hearers to "repentance for sins and faith in the blood of Jesus."[53]

The list of charges levied against Patrick Hamilton has been preserved in the *Acts and Monuments of the Christian Martyrs* by John Foxe and in the *Historie and Chronicles of Scotland* by Robert Lindesay of Piscottie. Sixteen specific accusations appear in the indictment, but it seems that Hamilton's doom was sealed by his response to the following seven concepts:

1. Man has no free will.
2. Justification is through faith in Christ alone.
3. Believers cannot attain to sinlessness while in this world.
4. A true Christian believes that he enjoys a state of grace before God.
5. Good works proceed from faith, but they do not make a person good.
6. Evil works proceed from an evil [sinful] nature. Repentance for sin absolves one from its just consequences.

50

7. Faith, hope, and charity are inseparable, so that a person cannot have one without the others.

To the above were added Hamilton's rejection of purgatory and oral confession to a priest, as well as the charge that he called the pope Antichrist.[54]

When the Roman Catholic authorities offered to spare Hamilton's life in return for a public recantation, the reformer replied,

As to my confession, I will not deny it for the fear of your fire, for my confession and belief is [sic] in Christ Jesus. Therefore I will not deny it. I will rather be content that my body burn in this fire for the confession of my faith in Christ, than my soul should burn in the fire of hell for denying the same.[55]

Several contemporaries described the death of Scotland's first Protestant martyr, and all agreed that it was a prolonged and painful ordeal. The official pronouncement that ordered the execution reads in part:

We, James, by the mercy of God, Archbishop of St. Andrews and Primate of Scotland, with the counsel, decree, and authority of the most revered Fathers in God, and Lords, Abbots, Doctors of Theology, Professors of Holy Scripture, and Masters of the University assisting us . . . in the cause of heretical pravity against Mr. Patrick Hamilton, being summoned to appear before us to answer to certain articles affirmed, taught, and preached by him,. . . have found the said Mr. Patrick in many ways inflamed with heresy, disputing, holding, and maintaining diverse heresies of Martin Luther . . . repugnant to our faith, and which is [sic] already condemned by general councils and most famous universities. . . .

We, having God and the integrity of our faith before our eyes,. . . condemn and define him to be punished by this our sentence,. . . to be deprived of all dignities, honours, orders, offices, and benefices of the Church,. . . and pronounce him to be delivered over to the secular power to be punished and his goods confiscated.[56]

The imposition of death by burning took place on 29 February 1528, and the ordeal lasted six hours, because a contrary wind and green wood kept the fire from becoming hot enough to consume the victim quickly. He was scorched but not burned until someone brought dry tinder and gun powder to finish the task. It was during the hours of Hamilton's suffering that Friar Alexander Campbell and others tormented him with pleas to invoke the aid of the Virgin Mary. The martyr remained, nevertheless, resolute to the end, praying for his enemies. His last recorded words were "Lord Jesus, receive my spirit. How long shall darkness overwhelm this realm? And how long will you [God] allow this tyranny of men."[57] The burning took place near the entrance to St. Salvatore's College, a spot now marked in the pavement with the initials "P.H."

Patrick Hamilton was not the only member of his family to be accused of heresy. His brother James and his sister Catherine were similarly charged about 1534. James fled to avoid prosecution but was excommunicated in absentia and suffered the confiscation of his possessions; Catherine recanted. The persecution, however, did not accomplish Beaton's goal of eradicating Protestant teaching in Scotland. On the contrary, it aroused considerable sympathy for Patrick Hamilton and great interest in evangelical doctrines, especially at St. Andrews University, where several friars then became outspoken in attacking corruption in the church.[58] Before long it became clear to Catholic authorities that many others were willing to take up the cause that Patrick Hamilton had been forced to lay down in death. As John Lindsay, an associate of Archbishop Beaton, said.

> My Lord, if you burn any more, unless you follow my counsel, you will utterly destroy yourselves. If you will burn them, let them be burned in deep cellars, for the smoke of Patrick Hamilton has infected as many as it blew upon.[59]

This may be a forgivable exaggeration, but it is undeniable that Hamilton had given vital momentum to the cause of reform, and his example inspired others to risk their lives in efforts to achieve it. As one modern interpreter has remarked about this reformer.

> By education and training he was academic. His chief appeal was to the educated and the high born; his method of argument was scholastic. The framework of his system was syllogistic, most effective in the classroom or the study. If the immediate outcome of his labors was small, at least he had influenced the men of rank and learning who best could scatter broadcast the truth they had learned from him.[60]

Patrick Hamilton was not an original thinker. As Lorimer put it so well, "He was a Lutheran, not a Luther,"[61] but he was an able exponent of the doctrines he had learned in Germany, and the courage he displayed in suffering for his convictions inspired heroism in others who came to embrace his teachings. From the time of Hamilton's death in 1527, to the return of George Wishart from the Continent in 1544, a small body of Lutherans worked to lay the foundation for the coming Protestant Church of Scotland. After 1544 Lutheranism was gradually supplanted by the Reformed faith, principally through the influence of John Calvin.

While it is clear that the major theological influences upon Patrick Hamilton came from Lutheran Germany, he never composed a systematic treatise on doctrine that expressed the entire body of distinctive Lutheran beliefs. On justification of *sola fide*, the bondage of man's sinful will, and the relationship of law and gospel he practically reproduced Luther's position. On the proper significance of the sacraments, however, a matter of great concern to Luther, Hamilton wrote nothing. At his trial he was not accused of denying the real presence of Christ in the Eucharist, which could be an indication that he espoused Luther's view. It is possible, nevertheless, that his association with William Tyndale and John Frith could have led him to adopt belief in the spiritual but not the physical presence of Christ in the sacrament. Tyndale especially wanted to prevent disagreement among the reformers from producing a rupture in Protestant ranks, but Luther was uncompromising in his defense of the real and physical presence of Christ.[62] Perhaps Hamilton shared the English reformer's concern for unity and deliberately refrained from espousing a position on this question. In any case, interpreters have nothing to evaluate but his silence.

Because of his status as a scholar and the social and political influence of his family, Patrick Hamilton was able to gain the attention of high-ranking lords, ecclesiastical and secular. Among the monks, those of the Augustinian order were more receptive to his teachings than were members of the Benedictine and Franciscan houses. Within a dozen years after his death a number of prominent citizens and officials of Edinburgh, Leith, Ayr, Stirling, Perth, St. Andrews, and Dundee had embraced the evangelical faith, and some of them, like Hamilton, gave their lives as martyrs, for it.[63]

Although Hamilton's career as a reformer was very brief, *Patrick's Places* was carried to various parts of the British Isles and continued to exert influence long after its author was dead. In 1536 John Gough, a book dealer in London, published a Protestant primer that appears to have been printed near Antwerp. Gough's name appeared on a list of printers issued by Cuthbert Tunstall, bishop of London, to warn against the circulation of Lutheran literature. Tunstall examined Gough but at that point concluded that he had been accused wrongly.

Careful analysis has shown, however, that Gough's primer is composed of materials borrowed from various Protestant sources, among them *Patrick's Places,* which Frith had rendered into English. Hamilton's work became a part of Gough's primer, and thereby the Scottish martyr helped to instruct English Protestants in the principles of the evangelical religion.[64] Patrick Hamilton, despite the brevity of his life and the violence of his death, became a significant figure in the history of British Protestantism, English as well as Scottish.

4

Scotland's Earliest Protestants

Soon after the word of Patrick Hamilton's death reached the University of Marburg, Francis Lambert exclaimed to his benefactor, Prince Philip of Hesse,

> He [Hamilton] came to your university out of Scotland, . . . and he returned to his country . . . to become its first, and now illustrious apostle. He was all on fire with zeal to confess the name of Christ, and he has offered himself to God as a holy, living sacrifice. He brought into the Church of God not only all of the splendor of his station and gifts, but his life itself. Such is the flower of surpassing sweetness, yes the ripe fruit, which your university has produced in its very commencement. You have not been disappointed of your wishes. You formed this school with the desire that from it might go forth intrepid confessors of Christ and steadfast assertors of his truth. See, you have one such already—an example in many ways illustrious. Others, if the Lord wills, will follow soon.[1]

Others did follow soon, and many of them came from St. Leonard's College, where scholars began to question Roman Catholic dogma and practices and to seek light from the Scriptures. As Knox related in his colloquial language,

> Within short space many began to call in doubt that which before they held for certain verity, in so much that the University of St. Andrews, and St. Leonard's College principally, . . . began to smell somewhat of the verity and to espy the vanity of the received superstition.[2]

Some of those who began criticizing the Roman church sought merely to promote a reform of morals and ecclesiastical administration and were not Protestant heretics. Sincere Catholics were disgusted with the condition of their church and sickened by the cruelty dealt to Patrick Hamilton. One of these was Friar William

Arth, who boldly assailed the immoralities of bishops, whom he accused of doing homage to "the master devil of hell, from whom such works and fruits do proceed." Arth, although a loyal Catholic, had to flee the wrath of the Scottish prelates. He went to England where he defended the prerogatives of the pope, much to the anger of Henry VIII, who put him in prison.[3]

While Arth and reformers of his persuasion sought a moral cleansing of their church, others worked as well for a revision of doctrine to conform to New Testament teachings. It appears that Alexander Seton (d. 1542) was one of the first to do so after the burning of Patrick Hamilton. A member of the Dominican Order of Preachers, this friar was father confessor to King James V. Knox, Spottiswoode, and Calderwood all regarded Seton as a preacher of Protestant doctrines as well as a critic of clerical corruption and abuses. During the season of Lent in 1527 he spoke out vigorously for the purification of the church, and in the process he revealed the Lutheran character of his beliefs. In one sermon he proclaimed

> that the law of God is the only law of righteousness; that, if God's law is not violated, no sin is committed; that it is not in man's power to satisfy for sin; and that the forgiveness of sin is not otherwise purchased than by unfeigned repentance and true faith apprehending the mercy of God in Christ.[4]

In his preaching Seton omitted any reference to the subjects of purgatory, fasting, veneration of saints, and works of righteousness, all of which constituted the typical subject matter of friars' sermons. Because of what he espoused on the question of slavation, and because of what he omitted in his preaching, he was accused of heresy.

Seton aggravated the episcopate by asserting that the Scriptures require bishops to be preachers of God's Word. He cited Isa. 56:9–12, which calls the leaders of Israel "dumb dogs" for living corruptly, and he contended that St. Paul taught that bishops must be teachers of God's people. When Archbishop Beaton took offense at Seton's preaching, the friar explained that he had not called anyone a dumb dog, he had merely recited what Isaiah had written.

This courageous friar did not spare the king in his preaching, and his criticisms of the royal immoralities made it easy for the archbishop to arouse the monarch against him. Confronted with the hostility of both the primate and the king, Seton fled to England, where he eventually became chaplain to the duke of Suffolk, a position he kept until his death.[5] He encountered clerical opposition in England too, where "the greatest matter laid against him was for preaching free justification by faith in Christ Jesus against false, confidence in good works and man's free will."[6]

About the same time that Alexander Seton left Scotland, Henry Forrest (d. ca. 1533) was arrested for defending Patrick Hamilton. Forrest, dean of the abbey of St. Colme's Inch, on the Isle of May in the Firth of Forth, came from Linlithgow and graduated from St. Leonard's College in 1526. He attended some of Patrick Hamilton's lectures and witnessed his execution. Forrest denied that Hamilton was a heretic, and as a consequence he too was charged with heresy. Friar Walter Laing examined him. When Laing asked him his opinion of Hamilton, Forrest replied "that he esteemed him to be a good man, and that the articles for which he was condemned might well be defended."[7] The accused related his opinion to Laing within the confessional box, where the priest was obliged to keep all matters confidential. Laing, however, broke the seal of confession and disclosed Forrest's statement, which was enough to condemn him.

After a period of incarceration Henry Forrest was executed near the abbey church in St. Andrews on a spot that could be seen from some distance. This, evidently, was done to make an example of him that would intimidate others. It, however, had the opposite effect of inspiring people to embrace the cause for which Forrest died.[8]

For some time before being apprehended, Forrest had been reading the works of St. Augustine. He served for a time as vicar at Dollar and there aroused episcopal censure for preaching each Sunday from Scripture. His bishop complained about Forrest's practice of teaching the Bible to laymen. When the vicar tried to show the benefits to be gained from such teaching, the bishop remarked that he knew little about the Bible except what he read in his breviary, a statement that led John Foxe to complain about another ignorant cleric, "You are like the Bishop of Dunkeld, who knew neither the new law nor the old."[9]

Unfortunately, information about Henry Forrest is scant, but it is much more abundant about Alexander Alesius (1500–65), who also became a disciple of Patrick Hamilton and thereby another link in the chain of Luther's Scottish connection.

Alesius (Alane) was educated at St. Andrews University and became a canon of the Augustinian priory there at a young age. He was one of the early students at St. Leonard's College, from which he received the bachelor of arts degree in 1515. In 1523 he studied with John Major at the university. As a canon he attempted to persuade Patrick Hamilton to renounce his heresy, but Alesius found the arguments of the accused irrefutable and, therefore, ceased his overtures.

Alesius's opposition to Hamilton reflected his hostility to heresy in general and to that of Martin Luther in particular. He gained fame by attacking the writings of the great German reformer, and in doing so drew on the arguments of the Englishman John Fisher, bishop of Rochester. His encounter with Hamilton, however, convinced Alesius that the Lutheran position could not be controverted easily. On the contrary, he found the doctrines of Luther increasingly attractive.

Because of his efforts against heresy, Alexander Alesius could have enjoyed the favor of the Scottish hierarchy indefinitely, but he aroused strong animosity instead by criticizing moral laxity among clergymen. The provost of St. Andrews took personal offense and had Alesius arrested along with some other canons who had likewise criticized him. Alesius was in prison about a year, until he was rescued by other canons while the provost was away. When the official returned, he arrested his critic again, but friends helped Alesius to escape to the Continent in 1532, and he wandered through Denmark, France, and Belgium until he arrived at Wittenberg toward the end of the year. His name Alesius means "wanderer" or "fugitive," and it appears that it was given to him by his German hosts.[10] He never returned to his homeland.

As a reformer in exile Alesius studied Lutheran theology carefully and subscribed eventually to the Augsburg Confession of Faith, composed by Philip Melanchthon as a statement of Lutheran doctrine for presentation to the diet of the Holy Roman Empire, which met at Augsburg in 1530. This confession is based on the German reformers' principle of *sola scriptura*, a concept that Alesius embraced heartily.

In 1533 Alesius published a treatise advocating the reading of the New Testament in the common tongues, which the prelates of Scotland had forbidden. He called on King James V to support him in the cause of ecclesiastical reform, and this led John Cochlaeus, a leading opponent of the Lutheran movement, to attack him. Cochlaeus replied to the arguments of Alesius in a treatise also addressed to the Scottish monarch and there contended that Melanchthon, not Alesius, was the real author of the appeal for royal approval of the vernacular New Testament. In the view of Cochlaeus, Bible reading might actually endanger the salvation of laymen who were not competent to understand it. He asked the king to enforce the decree of the bishops against the practice. James V agreed to do so. Although Alesius did not succeed in winning royal support for the circulation of the Scriptures, Tyndale's new Testament was being imported illegally from the Continent, and Catholic authorities were not able to prevent it.[11]

In 1535 Alexander Alesius went to England, where, for a while, he enjoyed the favor of Henry VIII at a time when the English king was negotiating for an alliance with the German Lutheran princes.[12] Alesius received a warm welcome from Thomas Cranmer, archbishop of Canterbury, to whom he presented a copy of Philip Melanchthon's *Loci Communes,* the first testbook on systematic theology composed by a Protestant scholar.[13]

Henry VIII made Alesius a royal scholar, and Thomas Cromwell, the king's chief minister, placed him as a reader in theology at Cambridge University. At Queen's College, Cambridge, Alesius delivered lectures on the Psalter, but despite his impressive scholarship, he encountered opposition from university professors who claimed that his teaching was heretical. Alesius had to return to London because the atmosphere became too hostile at Cambridge, and in London he married an English lady.

About the time of his return to London, Alesius was invited by Cromwell to speak to the Convocation of the Clergy against the Roman doctrine of the seven sacraments, a speech the Scot delivered with so much vigor that Cromwell and Cranmer found it prudent to silence him, lest he provoke the king, who had by no means renounced the Catholic religion despite his break with the Papacy. When Parliament passed the Act of Six Articles (1540), which forbade the clergy to marry, Alesius had to leave England. Cranmer, who lamented this deeply, gave him an expensive ring that had once belonged to Thomas Cardinal Wolsey to finance his flight.

Alesius went to Wittenberg for a brief stay after leaving England, and from there he went to Frankfurt an der Oder and then to Leipzig. He taught theology at Frankfurt for two years and then at the University of Leipzig, from which he received a doctor of theology degree and where he spent the last twenty-three years of his life. During this period he participated in several notewothy meetings with Protestant theologians such as Philip Melanchthon, Martin Bucer, reformer of Strassburg, and John Calvin.

Although Alexander Alesius adhered to the Lutheran reform and promoted its expansion, it appears that during the last decade of his life he deviated significantly from some of Luther's teachings. This became clear after Luther's death in 1546 left the German Protestant churches without a leader of his commanding stature. Melanchthon inherited Luther's mantle, but it soon became evident that he had developed reservations about some of Luther's doctrines. A dispute erupted within the church, which produced a struggle between the Philippists (followers of Melanchthon) and the Gnesio-Lutherans, who professed to uphold the original teachings of their late mentor. Alesius supported the Philippist party.

Philip Melanchthon was a rather sensitive and timid person who did not relish controversy but often found himself embroiled in it because of his support for Luther. Long after Luther had abandoned all hope for reforming the Catholic church, Melanchthon still cherished the prospect of reunited Christendom. He worked for many years toward that end only to find that he could achieve neither reconciliation with Rome nor lasting unity among Protestants. In contrast with Luther, who was adamant about points of theology that he deemed essential, Melanchthon was sometimes willing to make concessions in the interest of evangelical unity. This became apparent when Lutherans began to debate the relationship of good works to justification. An antinomian faction appeared within Lutheranism and disparaged good works so vehemently that a reaction was bound to occur. Those who opposed antinomianism, in turn, stressed the importance of good works so forcefully that they were accused of advocating synergism in justification. Because Melanchthon, by that time (ca. 1560), had come to reject Luther's position on the bondage of the unregenerate will, he did, in fact, avow synergism,[14] and Alesius supported that position.

Calvinists were especially critical of Lutherans who disparaged good works, though neither Luther nor Calvin did so. When the Philippists tried to show that they advocated good works, the Gnesio-Lutherans accused them of compromising with the Calvinists. Whatever the justice or injustice of this charge, it is true that Melanchthon and Alesius were eager to accommodate the Calvinists as much as possible in the interest of Protestant unity. These two reformers likewise showed tolerance toward the Reformed doctrine of the Lord's Supper, which clearly contradicted Luther's belief in the real and corporeal presence of Christ in the sacrament.[15]

Despite the deviations from Lutheran orthodoxy that Alesius displayed toward the end of his life, for most of his career as a reformer he was disciple of Martin Luther and of Patrick Hamilton, from whom he first learned of Luther's doctrine. Although he spent many years in exile, Alesius, through his writings, played an important part in the reform of the church in Scotland, and the major influence upon his beliefs was Lutheran in character.

Alexander Alesius was, of course, only one of a number of Scottish Protestants whose chief influence upon the Reformation was rendered from abroad. Another one was John Gau (d.ca. 1533), who holds the distinction of being Scotland's first Protestant systematic theologian. The exact place and date of Gau's birth are not known, but it appears that he was born in the last years of the fifteenth century, perhaps at St. Johnstown or at Perth. He enrolled at St. Andrews University about 1508 and received a bachelor of arts degree in 1510 and a master of arts degree in 1511 from St. Salvatore's College.

The particulars of Gau's life are few, but it is evident that he went to Denmark in 1533, perhaps to serve as minister to the Scots who resided there. Christian III, king of Denmark, embraced the Lutheran religion and defeated the rebellion of Catholic nobles in the struggle that ended in 1536. The monarch followed his triumph with a reform of his church. Catholic bishops who resisted the changes were imprisoned, and their revenues were diverted to the Crown. The Danish Parliament ratified the reforms, and John Bugenhagen, a co-worker of Martin Luther in Saxony, went to Denmark at the king's invitation to advise him on the pattern of reformation to be pursued. The plan adopted became known as the *Ordinatio Ecclesiastica*. Luther gave it his personal approval.[16]

John Gau was in Copenhagen during the years of religious strife, and while there he and John MacAlpine,[17] another Scottish Protestant, enjoyed the patronage of Denmark's Lutheran ruler. While still in the Danish city of Malmö (1533), Gau had published *The Right Way into the Kingdom of Heaven*, which was printed by John Hochstraten, an exile from Antwerp. Gau's treatise is the first thorough exposition of Luther's theology produced by a Scotsman.[18]

The Right Way expounds the Lutheran teaching on the Ten Commandments, the Apostles' Creed, and the Lord's Prayer, plus the angelic announcement to the Virgin Mary that she would become the mother of Christ (Luke 1:26–38). This was the typical format of Protestant catechisms intended for popular religious instruction. Both the structure and content of Gau's book are clearly Lutheran in character. The entire approach to the Christian faith is based on *sola scriptura*.[19] Salvation is affirmed to be *sola gratia*;[20] justification is *sola fide*;[21] man is portrayed as a depraved being by nature;[22] Christ is the sole head of the church;[23] and ecclesiastical authority is explained in terms in Luther's doctrine of the "keys" (Matt. 16:17–20).[24] The treatment of law and gospel is closely akin to that in *Patrick's Places*,[25] and parts of *The Right Way* reflect the influence of Luther's preface to the German New Testament and to the Epistle to the Romans in particular.[26] Even the language of composition in this work is Lutheran in style— bombastic.

Gau's *Right Way* is not an original work. His purpose was to reproduce Luther's teachings undiluted for the benefit of his countrymen. To accomplish this he composed an expansive translation of a work in Danish entitled *Den Rette Vey till Hiemmerigis Rige*, which had been written by Christiern Pedersen in 1531. Gau drew also upon the German edition of that book, which was the work of Urbanus Rhegius, a former Carmelite monk, who had proclaimed the reform in Augsburg.

Although he intended *The Right Way* for circulation in Scotland, it seems that Gau's design was frustrated, perhaps because Catholic authorities were able to seize and destroy most of the copies shipped there from the Continent. Gau's immediate influence on the Reformation in his homeland was therefore rather slight, so slight in fact that Knox, Spottiswoode, and Calderwood, the major historians of the era, did not even mention him.

A reformer considerably more effective in spreading Luther's teachings in Scotland was Henry Balnaves (ca. 1503–70). Born in Kirkcaldy, Balnaves was educated in philosophy in St. Salvatore's College, St. Andrews. He received a master of arts degree, perhaps from the University of Cologne, although no documentary evidence has been discovered to verify this tradition.[27] While in the Rhineland he studied law, and after he returned to Scotland, Balnaves became an official in the regency of James Hamilton, earl of Arran, who governed the kingdom for Mary, daughter of James V. While in the employ of the regent, Balnaves demonstrated sympathy and support for the reform of the church.

Lord Arran attempted to cement the position he had assumed upon the death of the king by arresting David Cardinal Beaton (1494–1546), nephew of Archbishop James Beaton, the primate of Scotland since 1539. Arran regarded David Beaton as a rival for control of the government. Since Beaton was Scotland's leading Catholic prelate, the opposition of the regent worked to the advantage of the Protestants. The regent allowed the preaching of evangelical doctrines, and at one point it appeared that a Lutheran triumph was in the making, Arran, however, did not remain true to the Protestant cause. In 1543, John Hamilton, abbot of Paisley and half brother of the regent, convinced Arran to return to the Catholic church. This led to repression of the Protestants, as Cardinal Beaton regained political influence and used it to persecute heretics. Protestant nobles began arming for defense, and the evangelical faith continued to spread. Prominent nobles, such as the earls of Glencairn and Errol, and William Lord Ruthven, supported the Protestant cause.[28]

Henry Balnaves emerged as a noteworthy reformer during the time when the earl of Arran was favorably disposed toward the evangelical position. After the regent returned to Roman Catholicism, Balnaves cast his lot with militants who had assassinated Cardinal Beaton in retaliation for his murder of George Wishart, who had brought the Helvetic Confession of Faith to Scotland from the Continent. Wishart was a Calvinist who had become a beloved friend of John Knox.[29]

Although he appears not to have been involved in the killing of Beaton, Balnaves joined the assassins in the castle at St. Andrews, where they took refuge after their crime.[30] By joining the rebels he, of course, became a marked man in the eyes of church and state. When the garrison surrendered, Balnaves became a prisoner of the French at Rouen, where he remained from 1547 to 1550. He did not return to Scotland for some time after 1550, and what he did in the interval is not clear.[31]

After he did go back to his homeland, Balnaves participated in a rebellion against Mary of Guise the queen mother, in 1559. He and the Protestant nobles, organized as the Lords of the Congregation of Jesus Christ, obtained financial and material aid for their resistance from Queen Elizabeth I. The English monarch promised to dispatch troops to aid in expelling the French forces that had been brought to Scotland by the queen mother, widow of James V, who had become regent for their daughter Mary Stuart, succeeding the earl of Arran in 1554. The Treaty of Berwick (1560) provided the needed English assistance, and within a few months the French forces were beaten. This effectively terminated French control over Scottish affairs. When the Scottish Parliament convened, it formed a provisional government in which the Protestants dominated. Parliament then proceeded to resolve the religious question by adopting the Scots Confession of Faith and by abolishing papal authority in the land and prohibiting celebration of the mass.

Because of his services to the Protestant movement, Henry Balnaves was honored by his comrades. He became lord of the session in 1563, and the General Assembly of the Kirk of Scotland appointed him to a commission directed to revise the *First Book of Discipline,* which had been designed to reorganize the national life of the kingdom on the basis of biblical principles.[32]

Although the Church of Scotland finally adopted the doctrinal position of John Calvin rather than that of Martin Luther, the first generation of Protestant reformers in Scotland absorbed a great deal of Lutheran influence, which continued to be significant despite the official embrace of Geneva rather than Wittenberg. It appears, for example, that Henry Balnaves owed a large debt to Luther, as well as to Knox, even though he participated in the Calvinist phase of the Scottish Reformation.

While a prisoner at Rouen (1548), Balnaves composed *The Con-*

fession of Faith, containing how the troubled man should seek refuge at his God, thereto led by faith: with the declaration of the articles of justification at length.[33] John Knox regarded this as a treatise of exceptional value and prepared it (with some revisions) for publication. The manuscript was lost for some time, however, and was not printed until 1584. Knox received the original while he was a prisoner at Rouen, where he had been taken along with other Protestants from the castle at St. Andrews. In commending this confession to readers Knox wrote,

> No man who comes with a goodly heart hereto, shall pass from the same without satisfaction. The firm and weak shall find strength and comfort; the rude and simple true knowledge and erudition; the learned and godly humbly rejoicing by the omnipotent spirit of Jesus Christ, to whom be glory before his congregation. Amen.[34]

The central theme of Balnaves's confession is justification through faith alone, which he expounded in a biblical-theological manner by tracing its appearances throughout Scripture, beginning with Genesis. His conception of the doctrine is typically Lutheran in character, and it bears marked similarities to Luther's treatment of that subject in his 1535 commentary on Galatians. At points Balnaves seems almost to quote Luther.[35] Since John Knox gave this confession his enthusiastic endorsement and added a few revisions, it is evident that he, like Balnaves, owed some debt to Luther.

As Knox indicated, Belnaves addressed three principal concerns: (1) how sinful man should seek refuge with God; (2) how faith in Christ justifies a sinner; and (3) how good works follow faith as its inevitable fruits. Like Luther, Balnaves regarded justification through faith alone as the grand theme of the Bible and the cornerstone of all Christian belief about salvation:

> The substance of the Article of Justification is to cleave and stick fast to our God, knowing him our Maker . . . and to believe firmly, undoubtedly, that we are not righteous nor just by ourselves, nor yet by our own works, which are less than little, but by the help of another—the only begotten Son of God, Jesus Christ, who has delivered and redeemed us from death, the devil, and sin, and has given to us eternal life.[36]

Balnaves based his doctrine of justification on his understanding of fallen man's spiritual condition, which, he contended, is one of depravity and slavery to sin. He assailed those who believed they could please God by free will and natural reason, and he labeled idolaters all who trust in their works and religious ceremonies. He argued that denial of *sola fide* is satanic in origin—a devilish device employed by sinners ever since the fall.[37] Christ and the prophets and the apostles were persecuted for proclaiming *sola fide,* and, Balnaves asserted, Roman Catholic prelates likewise were persecuting true preachers of the gospel.[38]

In order to illustrate his argument biblically, Henry Balnaves cited numerous examples of believers who disavowed personal righteousness and trusted in the mercy of God alone. Among the figures he mentioned were Abraham, Job, and David:

> Abraham, in his father's house, an idolater as he was, and the rest of his house, made no good cause to God or merit to obtain the promise that he should be the father of all the faithful; but [he] only believed in the promise of God. . . . But even as they [Abraham and his household] were accepted as righteous through faith without all their merits or deserts, so shall we be who are the sons of Abraham and heirs of the promise.[39]

Job too, in Balnaves's view, was justified through faith alone. Although God hailed him as a just man, Job's righteousness was not of a quality that could win the divine favor. He was just when compared with other men, but he was still a sinner before God, as he confessed at the close of his book: "I despise myself and repent in dust and ashes" (Job 42:6). King David, called a "man after God's own heart" (1 Sam. 13:14), placed no confidence in his works but prayed, "Do not bring your servant into judgment, for no one living is righteous before you" (Ps. 143:2). Through faith the king of Israel trusted in the mercy of God.[40] Even Old Testament saints, then, were justified through faith alone, a truth understood by church fathers such as St. Augustine and St. Bernard of Clairvaux.[41]

To rebut the arguments of those who contended that obedience to God's laws merits salvation, Balnaves asserted that the accusations of the law are intended to drive sinners to Christ for forgiveness,[42] and he invoked the Lutheran distinction between law and gospel to fortify his case.

> The office of the law is to accuse the wicked, make them afraid, and condemn them as transgressors of the same. The office of Christ is to

preach mercy, remission of sins, freely in his blood, through faith give consolation, and to save sinners.[43]

The law requires perfect obedience; but no one except Christ has ever rendered such obedience. Therefore man cannot attain to righteous standing before God by performing works of the law. Justification then is

> a thing far above all law, either of God or man; for it is the righteousness by which a wicked man is made righteous through faith in the blood of Jesus Christ, without the works of the law, because "by the deeds of the law no flesh shall be made righteous before God," as the apostle [Paul] said (Galatians 2:16).[44]

Balnaves defined justifying faith as a "gift from God, . . . the instrument by which we obtain the mercy of God, remission of our sins, the gift of the Holy Spirit, and everlasting life, all for Christ's sake, without our deserts."[45] Just as "the sick man receives his health, the poor man his alms, and the dry earth the rain, all without their merits or deserts, so you [Christians] receive this righteousness from God."[46]

Like practically all Protestant theologians of his day, Balnaves believed that the gift of justifying faith is granted only to God's elect, or chosen, people. Like Luther, he had no patience with those who objected that this was unfair. Balnaves alleged that those who dare to question God show themselves to be "the serpent's seed, from whom they learned that lesson."[47]

Whenever the doctrine of justification *sola fide* was published, it was almost inevitable that Roman Catholic rejoinders would appear in the form of a complaint that this teaching disparages good works and promotes moral irresponsibility. Luther responded to this challenge by arguing that true Christian faith produces love, for faith is always active in love, which is the theme of his great treatise *The Freedom of a Christian*.[48] Balnaves dealt with criticism in the same way, contending that genuine faith always produces good works. It cannot be idle, but must be active in generating deeds of charity. Before one can do good works, however, he must be justified through faith, for "the faithful and righteous man brings forth . . . good works to the honor and glory of God and the profit of his neighbor, which [works] bear witness of his inward faith and testify before men that he is righteous."[49] Those who claim to be justified but fail to perform good works deceive themselves. They have a merely "historical" rather than a personal faith in Christ.[50]

Balnaves was as adamant as Luther in asserting that good works are the fruits of faith, and like Luther he, too, insisted that neither works performed before nor after faith contribute to justification.[51]

Together with all Protestant reformers, Balnaves sought to cleanse the church of corruption and abuses as well as to reform its doctrines. He therefore attacked such practices as prayers to images and seeking the intercession of departed saints, and he failed against masses, clerical celibacy, purgatory, holy water, compulsory fasting, and the institution of monasticism.[52] Since the ecclesiastical leaders had resisted pleas for reform, he called upon the civil authorities to take the lead in abolishing false religion. He said this was their Christian vocation, and he cited Old Testament rulers as examples to follow. Balnaves here seems to have echoed Luther's call to the princes of Germany.[53]

In his doctrine of salvation Henry Balnaves seems to have echoed Luther's teaching in every aspect but one—the extent of Christ's atonement. Luther believed that Christ died for everyone, although only the elect would avail themselves of the redeeming benefits of his sacrificial death.[54] Balnaves, however, appears to have narrowed the design of the atonement to the elect alone, in the manner of many Calvinist theologians. In denouncing all reliance on human works for salvation Balnaves wrote:

> They who think faith not sufficient to justify without works, but will have their own good deeds joined to help in their justification, these are they who go astray from Christ and would be equal with him in their own justification. *For none of these has Christ suffered death.*[55]

Balnaves taught that Christ "has shed his blood for all who believe in him," and he explained that this was an atonement for all people without distinction as to race, sex, social standing, and the like, but not for everyone without exception.[56]

The career of Henry Balnaves then may indicate that the process of transition in the Scottish Reformation from its Lutheran foundations to the Calvinism of its maturity was underway at least as early as 1548, when Balnaves composed his confession of faith.

Luther's writings, however, continued to circulate widely in the kingdom and thereby to exert significant influence upon the development of Scottish Protestantism. During the decade of the 1540s the hymnal *Gude and Godlie Ballatis,* which was compiled by John and Robert Wedderburn, gained considerable popularity as a vehicle of devotion, and its theological character is Lutheran. This is the earliest known metrical work in the Scottish dialect, and its compilers were associated as students with St. Andrews University, where Robert received the bachelor and master of arts degrees from St. Leonard's College. John appears to have attended the University of Wittenberg, at least for a brief time.[57]

5

Conclusion

Despite the great influence that Martin Luther exerted upon Scotland's earliest Protestants, the German reformer did not long remain the major teacher of Scottish evangelicals. After about 1544, when George Wishart returned to his homeland, Swiss rather than German ideas of reform achieved a commanding position there. Zwinglian and Calvinist teachers built upon the Lutheran foundation, and the Reformed faith became ascendant rather rapidly.

Exactly why Lutheranism receded so quickly is difficult to ascertain, but, as one recent interpreter has observed, the Lutheran movement flourished where it enjoyed the support of powerful princes, which it did not receive in Scotland. Calvinism, on the contrary, did not seem to require such support in order to prosper.[1]

The doctrinal passage from Lutheran to Reformed teachings may have begun when Wishart translated the First Helvetic Confession of Faith of 1526 into the Scottish dialect. This systematic treatment of Christian dogma gained wide acceptance in Scotland and thereby helped to promote the Swiss brand of reform. No comparable Lutheran confession was current in the kingdom at that time. When John Knox embraced the Reformed theology and invested his dynamic personality in its service, that persuasion proved to be practically irresistible. The success of the Reformed movement (principally Calvinism), however, did not mean the eradication of Lutheran influences in Scotland, despite the absence of an organized Lutheran church in the country.

Although Knox eventually became a Calvinist, he never renounced Luther, and he continued to espouse the fundamental

70

teachings of the German reformer that Patrick Hamilton had introduced. Early in his career Knox had been influenced by Luther's writings, as his publication of Balnaves's work on justification bears witness. "Lutheran influence was strong and probably predominant in Knox's doctrine of justification by faith,"[2] even though Calvin and all major Protestant reformers also espoused it. This appears to be the case with the doctrine of predestination as well, for Knox's *On Predestination, in Answer to the Cavillations by an Anabaptist* (1560) bears a striking resemblance to Luther's *Bondage of the Will* (1525).[3] Knox's manner of argumentation corresponds to that of Luther rather than to Calvin's method, although the beliefs of all three of these reformers were, on this subject, practically identical. Knox's concern in defending and explaining the doctrine of predestination was soteriological, as he related the doctrine to his own conversion to Christ. Like Luther, he was concerned about the assurance of salvation, and he based his assurance upon God's eternal decree of election.[4]

The most conspicuous disagreement between Lutheran and Reformed theologians in the sixteenth century pertained to the sacraments, especially to the Lord's Supper. Lutherans believed in the real and *corporeal* presence of Christ in the Eucharist, while Calvinists contended for a real but merely *spiritual* presence. Knox did not begin any serious study of Calvin's writings until he was in England (1549), where he remained until Mary Tudor (1553–58) came to the throne. He then left for Geneva, where he enjoyed a close relationship with Calvin. In November 1554, at Calvin's urging, Knox accepted the pastorate of an English refugee congregation at Frankfort am Main, and while in Germany he had ample opportunities to associate with Lutherans. This exposure to Lutheran teachings may have been highly significant in developing Knox's understanding of the Eucharist, an understanding that seems to reflect the lingering influence of Luther's teaching.

When Knox presented a summary of his teaching on the sacraments in 1550, he depicted the Eucharist as a means whereby God is gracious to the recipients. He did not portray it as something believers do for God. He contended that, in this sacrament, Christ gathers his people to himself in one visible body. This sacrament then portrays Christians as members of Christ's body, the body of which he is the head. This was a singular teaching among Reformed theologians at that time. It assigns far greater significance to the sacrament than Calvin was willing to do. Knox believed that the church is established on the Word and the sacraments.[5]

When the Church of Scotland adopted its confession in 1560, it denounced the view of Zwingli that the bread and wine in the Eucharist are mere symbols of Christ's body and blood, and it affirmed belief in the real presence of Christ, although not in the Lutheran understanding of the term. The confession states categorically, "We utterly damn the vanity of those who affirm the sacraments to be nothing else but naked and bare signs." It then goes on to affirm that believers "eat the body and drink the blood of the Lord Jesus," even though his literal body ascended to heaven in the first century.[6] Knox was the chief author of the Scots Confession, and its strong emphasis upon the role of the Eucharist probably reflects the ongoing influence of Luther's teaching on his thinking about this subject. On the central doctrines of *sola scriptura, sola gratia,* and *sola fide,* Knox, like earlier reformers, was one with Luther, and on the Lord's Supper his emphasis was closer to Luther's position in some ways than to that of Calvin.

In addition to the realm of theological literature, Luther's influence endured in Scotland through hymnody, for the triumph of the Reformed persuasion did not bring the elimination of earlier ballads and hymns for which Luther's teachings were the inspiration. Scots continued to sing the *Guide and Godlie Ballatis* that the Lutheran Wedderburn brothers had composed.

Finally, even Roman Catholicism itself became something of a conduit through which Lutheran concepts flowed across Scotland. This was so because Archbishop John Hamilton (ca. 1511–71), who succeeded David Cardinal Beaton as primate of the kingdom, attempted to blunt the advance of Protestantism by sponsoring a few measures for the internal reform of his own church. In doing so he authorized publication of a catechism that ever since has been associated with his name, even though he was not the actual compiler. This manual, which was intended primarily for the instruction of ignorant clerics, emphasized the need for the study of the Bible, and on the matter of justification its teaching is remarkably close to the Lutheran doctrine. The catechism defines the church as the assembly of believers that is responsible for the proper administration of the Word of God and the sacraments.

No mention appears in this document of the Papacy as being essential in the true church.[7]

Whatever the archbishop may have hoped to achieve by issuing this noteworthy volume, it had very little effect in retarding the spread of Protestantism. Since the prelate himself was notorious for his immoralities, a book so closely identified with his name could not acquire great popularity. Those who did read it, however, were in a position to gain glimpses of Lutheran teaching, even though the catechism was intended to rebut the evangelical cause. It is one of the great ironies of the religious controversy that a document designed to defend Catholicism contributed at least a little to the dissemination of teachings it was issued to thwart.

John Knox went to Geneva in 1555 and stayed there until 1559 in a community that he described as "the most perfect school of Christ that ever was in the earth since the days of the apostles."[8] Under the influence of Calvin and other Reformed theologians, he consolidated his thinking about doctrinal issues and emerged from the experience committed to the Genevan version of Protestantism. His passage from Lutheranism to Calvinism was, nevertheless, without any conscious or deliberate rejection of the former. Knox placed the stamp of Calvinism firmly upon the Church of Scotland, but the church he helped to establish was erected upon foundations laid by the first generation of Scottish Protestants, many of whom were links in the chain of Luther's Scottish connection.

Appendix

A BRIEF TREATISE OF MASTER PATRICK HAMILTON CALLED

PATRICK'S PLACES

Translated into English by John Frith with a preface by the same

John Frith unto the Christian Reader.

Blessed be God, the Father of our Lord Jesus Christ, who in these last days and perilous times hath stirred up in all countries witnesses unto his Son, to testify the truth unto the unfaithful, to save at least some from the snares of Antichrist, which lead to perdition, as ye may here perceive by that excellent and well learned young man, Patrick Hamilton, born in Scotland of a noble progeny: who, to testify the truth, sought all means, and took upon him priesthood (even as Paul circumcised Timothy, to win the weak Jews), that he might be admitted to preach the pure word of God. Notwithstanding, as soon as the chamberlain and other bishops of Scotland had perceived that the light began to shine, which disclosed their falsehood which they conveyed in darkness, they laid hands on him, and because he would not deny his Savior Christ at their instance, they burnt him to ashes. Nevertheless, God of his bounteous mercy (to publish to the whole world what a man these monsters have murdered), hath reserved a little treatise, made by this Patrick, which if ye list, ye may call Patrick's Places: for it treateth exactly of certain common places,

John Foxe, *Acts and Monuments,* ed. Stephen Reed Cattley (1843–49; reprint, New York: AMS Press, Inc., 1965), 4:563–78.

74

which known, ye have the pith of all divinity. This treatise I have turned into the English tongue, to the profit of my nation: to whom I beseech God to give light, that they may espy the deceitful paths of perdition, and return to the right way, which leadeth to life everlasting, Amen.

THE DOCTRINE OF THE LAW

The law is a doctrine that biddeth good, and forbiddeth evil, as the commandments do specify here following.

The Ten Commandments of God.

1. Thou shalt worship but one God.
II. Thou shalt make thee no image to worship it.
III. Thou shalt not swear by his name in vain.
IV. Hold the Sabbath day holy.
V. Honour thy father and thy mother.
VI. Thou shalt not kill.
VII. Thou shalt not commit adultery.
VIII. Thou shalt not steal.
IX. Thou shalt not bear false witness.
X. Thou shalt not desire ought that belongeth to thy neighbor.

All these commandments are briefly comprised in these two, hereunder ensuing: 'Love thy Lord God with all thine heart, with all thy soul, and with all thy mind: this is the first, and great commandment. The second is like unto this, that is, Love thy neighbour as thyself. On these two commandments hang all the law and the prophets.'

CERTAIN GENERAL PROPOSITIONS PROVED BY THE SCRIPTURE.

The First Proposition.

'He that loveth God loveth his neighbour.'
This proposition is proved by 1 John iv.: 'If a man say, I love God, and yet hateth his brother, he is a liar. He that loveth not his

brother whom he hath seen, how can he love God whom he hath not seen?'

The Second Proposition.

'He that loveth his neighbour as himself, keepeth all the commandments of God.'

This proposition is proved: 'Whatsoever ye would that men should do to you, even so do to them: for this is the law and the prophets.' 'He that loveth his neighbour, fulfilleth the law. Thou shalt not commit adultery: thou shalt not kill: thou shalt not steal: thou shalt not bear false witness: thou shalt not desire,' &c. 'And if there be any other commandment, all are comprehended in this saying, Love thy neighbour as thyself,' 'All the law is fulfilled in one word, that is, Love thy neighbour as thyself.'

ARGUMENT.

He that loveth his neighbour, keepeth all the commandments of God.

He that loveth God, loveth his neighbour.

Ergo, he that loveth God, keepeth all the commandments of God.

The Third Proposition.

'He that hath faith, loveth God.'

'My Father loveth you, because you love me, and believe that I come of God.'

ARGUMENT.

He that keepeth the commandments of God, hath the love of God.

He that hath faith, keepeth the commandments of God.

Ergo, he that hath faith, loveth God.

The Fourth Proposition.

'He that keepeth one commandment of God, keepeth them all.'
This proposition is confirmed: 'It is impossible for a man with-

out faith to please God;' that is, to keep any one of God's commandments, as he should do. Then whosoever keepeth any one commandment, hath faith.

He that hath faith keepeth all the commandments of God.
He that keepeth any one commandment of God, hath faith.
Ergo, he that keepeth one commandment, keepeth them all.

The Fifth Proposition.

'He that keepeth not all the commandments of God, keepeth not one of them.'

He that keepeth one commandment of God, keepeth all.
Ergo, he that keepeth not all the commandments of God,
    keepeth not one of them.

The Sixth Proposition.

'It is not in our power to keep any one of the commandments of God.'

It is impossible to keep any of the commandments of God,
    without grace.
It is not in our power to have grace.
Ergo, it is not in our power to keep any of the
    commandments of God.
And even so may you reason concerning the Holy Ghost and faith, forasmuch as neither without them we are able to keep any of the commandments of God, nor yet be they in our power to have: *Non est volentis neque currentis*, &c.

The Seventh Proposition.

'The law was given us to show our sin.'
'By the law cometh the knowledge of sin,' 'I knew not what sin meant, but through the law; for I had not known what lust had

meant, except the law had said, Thou shalt not lust. Without the law sin was dead, that is, it moved me not, neither wist I that it was sin, which notwithstanding was sin, and forbidden by the law.

The Eighth Proposition.

The law biddeth us do that thing which is impossible for us.

ARGUMENT.

The keeping of the commandments is to us impossible.

The law commandeth to us the keeping of the commandments.

Ergo, the law commandeth unto us what is impossible.

Objection: But thou wilt say, 'Wherefore doth God bid us do what is impossible for us?'

Answer: I answer, to make thee know that thou art but evil, and that there is no remedy to save thee in thine own hand: and thou mayest seek remedy at some other; for the law doth nothing else but command thee.

THE DOCTRINE OF THE GOSPEL.

The Gospel is as much as to say, in our tongue, good tidings; like as these be hereunder following, and such others. Luke ii.

Christ is the Saviour of the world. John iv.

Christ is the Saviour. Luke ii.

Christ died for us. Rom. v.

Christ died for our sins. Rom. iv.

Christ bought us with his blood. 1 Pet. ii.

Christ washed us with his blood. Apoc. i.

Christ offered himself for us. Gal. i.

Christ bare our sins on his back. Isa. liii.

Christ came into this world to save sinners. 1 Tim. i.

Christ came into this world to take away our sins. 1 John iii.

Christ was the price that was given for us and our sins. 1 Tim. ii.

Christ was made debtor for us. Rom. viii.

Christ hath payed our debt, for he died for us. Col. ii.

Christ made satisfaction for us and our sins. 1 Cor. vii.

Christ is our righteousness. 1 Cor. i.

Christ is our sanctification. 1 Cor. i.
Christ is our redemption. Eph. ii.
Christ is our peace. Rom. v.
Christ hath pacified the Father of heaven for us. 1 Cor. iii.
Christ is ours and all his. Col. ii.
Christ hath delivered us from the law, from the devil, and from hell. 1 John i.

The Father of heaven hath forgiven us our sins, for Christ's sake.

(Or any such other, like to the same, which declare unto us the mercy of God.)

The Nature and Office of the Law and of the Gospel.

The law showeth us our sin. Rom. iii.
The gospel showeth us remedy for it. John i.
The law showeth us our condemnation. Rom. vii.
The gospel showeth us our redemption. Col. i.
The law is the word of ire. Rom. iv.
The gospel is the word of grace. Acts xx.
The law is the word of despair. Deut. xxvii.
The gospel is the word of comfort. Luke ii.
The law is the word of unrest. Rom. vii.
The gospel is the word of peace. Eph. vi.

A Disputation between the Law and the Gospel; where is shown the difference or contrariety between them both.

The law saith, 'Pay thy debt.'
The gospel saith, 'Christ hath paid it.'
The law saith, 'Thou art a sinner; despair, and thou shalt be damned.'
The gospel saith, 'Thy sins are forgiven thee, be of good comfort, thou shalt be saved!'
The law saith, 'Make amends for thy sins.'
The gospel saith, 'Christ hath made it for thee.'
The law saith, 'The Father of heaven is angry with thee.'
The gospel saith, 'Christ hath pacified him with his blood.'

The law saith, 'Where is thy righteousness, goodness, and satisfaction?'

The law saith,'Christ is thy righteousness, thy goodness, thy satisfaction.'

The law saith, 'Thou art bound and obliged to me, to the devil, and to hell.'

The gospel saith, 'Christ hath delivered thee from them all.'

THE DOCTRINE OF FAITH

Faith is to believe God, like as Abraham believed God, and it was imputed unto him for righteousness.

To believe God, is to believe his word, and to account it true, that he saith.

He that believeth not God's word, believeth not God himself.

He that believeth not God's word, counteth him false and a liar, and believeth not that he may and will fulfil his word; and so he denieth both the might of God, and God himself.

The Ninth Proposition.

'Faith is the gift of God.'

ARGUMENT.

Every good thing is the gift of God.
Faith is good.
Ergo, faith is the gift of God.

The Tenth Proposition.

Faith is not in our power.

ARGUMENT.

The gift of God is not in our power.
Faith is the gift of God.
Ergo, faith is not in our power.

The Eleventh Proposition.

He that lacketh faith, cannot please God.

'Without faith it is impossible to please God;' 'all that cometh not of faith is sin; for without faith can no man please God.'

INDUCTION.

He that lacketh faith, trusteth not God: he that trusteth not God, trusteth not his word: he that trusteth not his word, holdeth him false and a liar: he that holdeth him false and a liar, believeth not that he may do that he promiseth, and so denieth he that he is God.

Ergo, a *primo ad ultimum,* he that lacketh faith cannot please God.

If it were possible for any man to do all the good deeds that ever were done either by men or angels, yet being in this case, it is impossible for him to please God.

The Twelfth Proposition.

All that is done in faith, pleaseth God.

Right is the word of God, and all his works in faith.

Lord, thine eyes look to faith: that is as much as to say, Lord, thou delightest in faith.

The Thirteenth Proposition.

He that hath faith is just and good.

ARGUMENT.

He that is a good tree, bringing forth good fruit, is just and good.

He that hath faith, is a good tree bringing forth good fruit.

Ergo, he that hath faith, is just and good.

The Fourteenth Proposition.

He that hath faith, and believeth God, cannot displease him.

INDUCTION.

He that hath faith, believeth God; he that believeth God, believeth his word; he that believeth his word, wotteth well that he is

81

true and faithful, and may not lie, knowing that he both may, and will, fulfil his word.

Ergo, a *primo ad ultimum,* he that hath faith cannot displease God, neither can any man do a greater honour to God, than to count him true.

OBJECTION.

Thou wilt then say, that theft, murder, adultery, and all vices please God.

ANSWER.

Nay verily, for they cannot be done in faith; for 'a good tree beareth good fruit.'

The Fifteenth Proposition.

Faith is a certainty of assuredness.
'Faith is a sure confidence of things which are hoped for, and certainty of things which are not seen.'
'The same Spirit certifieth our spirit, that we are the children of God.'
Moreover, he that hath faith, wotteth well that God will fulfil his word: whereby it appeareth, that faith is a certainty of assuredness.

A MAN IS JUSTIFIED BY FAITH

'Abraham believed God, and it was imputed unto him for righteousness.'
'We suppose therefore, that a man is justified by faith, without the deeds of the law.'
'He that worketh not, but believeth on him that justifieth the wicked, his faith is counted to him for righteousness.'
'The just man liveth by his faith.'
'We wot that a man is not justified by the deeds of the law, but by the faith of Jesus Christ; and we believe in Jesus Christ, that we may be justified by the faith of Christ, and not by the deeds of the law.'

WHAT IS THE FAITH OF CHRIST?

The faith of Christ is to believe in him; that is, to believe his word, and believe that he will help thee in all thy need, and deliver thee from all evil.

Thou wilt ask me, 'What word?' I answer, 'The gospel.'

'He that believeth in Christ shall be saved.' Mark xvi.

'He that believeth the Son hath everlasting life.' John iii.

'Verily I say unto you, he that believeth in me, hath everlasting life.' John vi.

'This I write unto you, that you believe on the Son of God, that ye may know how that ye have eternal life.' 1 John v.

'Thomas! because thou hast seen me, therefore hast thou believed: happy are they which have not seen, and yet have believed in me.' John xxii.

'All the prophets to him bear witness, that whosoever believeth in him shall have remission of their sins.' Acts x.

'What must I do that I may be saved?' The apostles answered, 'Believe in the Lord Jesus Christ, and thou shalt be saved.' Acts xvi.

'If thou dost acknowledge with thy mouth that Jesus is the Lord, and believe with thine heart that God raised him from death, thou shalt be safe.' Rom. x.

'He that believeth not in Christ shall be condemned. He that believeth not the Son shall never see life, but the ire of God bideth upon him.' John iii.

'The Holy Ghost shall reprove the word of sin, because they believe not in me.' John xvi.

They that believe in Jesus Christ are the sons of God. 'Ye are all the sons of God, because ye believe in Jesus Christ.' 1 John iii.

'He that believeth that Christ is the Son of God, is safe.' John i.

'Peter said, Thou art Christ the Son of the living God! Jesus answered and said unto him, Happy art thou, Simon, the son of Jonas, for flesh and blood hath not opened to thee that, but my Father that is in heaven.' Matt. xvi.

'We have believed, and know that thou art Christ the Son of the living God.'

'I believe that thou art Christ the Son of God, which should come into the world.' John xi.

'These things are written, that ye might believe that Jesus is Christ the Son of God, and that ye, in believing, might have life.' John xx.

'I believe that Jesus is the Son of God.' Acts viii.

The Sixteenth Proposition.

'He that believeth the gospel, believeth God.'

He that believeth God's word, believeth God.
The gospel is God's word.
Ergo, he that believeth the gospel, believeth God.
To believe the gospel is this: that Christ is the Saviour of the world.' John vi.
Christ is our Saviour. Luke ii.
Christ bought us with his blood. Heb. xiii. 1 Pet. i. Apoc. v.
Christ washed us with his blood. Apoc. i.
Christ offered himself for us. Heb. ix.
Christ bare our sins on his own back, &c. 1 Pet. ii.

The Seventeenth Proposition.

'He that believeth not the gospel believeth not God.'

ARGUMENT.

He that believeth not God's word, believeth not God himself.
The gospel is God's word.
Ergo, he that believeth not the gospel, believeth not God
    himself; and consequently, he that
believeth not those things above written, and such others,
    believeth not God.

The Eighteenth Proposition.

He that believeth the gospel, shall be safe.
'Go ye into all the world, and preach the gospel unto every creature: he that believeth and is baptized, shall be saved; but he that believeth not, shall be condemned.' Mark xvi.

A COMPARISON BETWEEN FAITH AND INCREDULITY.

Faith is the root of all good: incredulity is the root of all evil.
Faith maketh God and man good friends: incredulity maketh them foes.

Faith bringeth God and man together: incredulity sundereth them.

All that faith doth, pleaseth God: all that incredulity doth, displeaseth God.

Faith only maketh a man good and righteous: incredulity only maketh him unjust and evil.

Faith maketh a man a member of Christ: incredulity maketh him a member of the devil.

Faith maketh a man the inheritor of heaven: incredulity maketh him inheritor of hell.

Faith maketh a man the servant of God: incredulity maketh him the servant of the devil.

Faith showeth us God to be a sweet father: incredulity showeth him a terrible judge.

Faith holdeth stiff by the word of God: incredulity wavereth here and there.

Faith counteth and holdeth God to be true: incredulity holdeth him false and a liar.

Faith knoweth God: incredulity knoweth him not.

Faith loveth both God and his neighbour: incredulity loveth neither of them.

Faith only saveth us: incredulity only condemneth us.

Faith extolleth God and his deeds: incredulity extolleth herself and her own deeds.

OF HOPE.

Hope is a trusty looking after the thing that is promised us to come, as we hope after the everlasting joy, which Christ that promised unto all that believe in him.

We should put our hope and trust in God alone, and in no other thing.

'It is good to trust in God and not in man.' Psalm cxviii.

'He that trusteth in his own heart is a fool.' Prov. xxviii.

'It is good to trust in God, and not in princes.' Psalm cxviii.

'They shall be like unto the images which they make, and all that trust in them.' Psalm cxv.

'He that trusteth in his own thoughts doth ungoldly.' Prov. xii.

'Cursed is he that trusteth in man.' Jer. xvii.

'Bid the rich men of this world, that they trust not in their unstable riches, but that they trust in the living God.' 1 Tim. vi.

'It is hard for them that trust in money, to enter into the kingdom of heaven.'

Moreover we should trust in him only, that may help us: God only may help us, therefore we should trust in him only.

'Well are they that trust in God, and woe to them that trust not in him.'

'Well is that man that trusteth in God, for God shall be his trust.'

'He that trusteth in him, shall understand the verity.' Wis. iii.

'They shall rejoice that trust in thee; they shall ever be glad, and thou wilt defend them.' Psalm v.

OF CHARITY,

Charity is the love of thy neighbour. The rule of charity is this: Do as thou wouldst be done to: for Christ holdeth all alike, the rich, the poor, the friend and the foe, the thankful and un-thankful, the kinsman and stranger.

A Comparison between Faith, Hope, and Charity.

Faith cometh of the word of God; hope cometh of faith; and charity springeth of them both.

Faith believeth the word; hope trusteth after that which is promised by the word; charity doth good unto her neighbour, through the love that she hath to God, and gladness that is within herself.

Faith looketh to God and his word; hope looketh unto his gift and reward; charity looketh on her neighbour's profit.

Faith receiveth God; hope receiveth his reward; charity loveth her neighbour with a glad heart, and that without any respect of reward.

Faith pertaineth to God only; hope to his reward; and charity to her neighbour.

THE DOCTRINE OF WORKS.

No manner of Works make us righteous.

'We believe that a man shall be justified without works.' Rom. iii.

'No man is justified by the deeds of the law, but by the faith of

86

Jesus Christ; and we believe in Jesus Christ, that we may be justified by the faith of Christ, and not by the deeds of the law; for if righteousness come by the law, then died Christ in vain.' Gal. ii.

'That no man is justified by the law is manifest; for a righteous man liveth by this faith, but the law is not of faith.' Acts xvii.

Moreover, since Christ the maker of heaven and earth, and all that is therein, behoved to die for us, we are compelled to grant that we were so far drowned and sunken in sin, that neither our deeds, nor all the treasures that ever God made or might make, could have holpen us out of them, therefore no deeds or works may make us righteous.

No Works make us unrighteous.

If any evil works make us unrighteous; then the contrary works should make us righteous. But it is proved that no works can make us righteous: therefore no works make us unrighteous.

Works make us neither good nor evil.

It is proved that works neither make us righteous nor unrighteous: therefore no works make us either good or evil. For righteous and good are one thing, and unrighteous and evil likewise one.

Good works make not a good man, nor evil works an evil man: but a good man bringeth forth good works, and an evil man evil works.

Good fruit maketh not the tree good, nor evil fruit the tree evil: but a good tree beareth good fruit, and an evil tree evil fruit.

A good man cannot do evil works, nor an evil man good works: for a good tree cannot bear evil fruit, nor an evil tree good fruit.

A man is good ere he do good works, and evil ere he do evil works: for the tree is good, ere it bear good fruit, and evil, ere it bear evil fruit.

Every man, and the works of man, are either good or evil.

Every tree, and the fruits thereof, are either good or evil. 'Either make ye the tree good, and the fruit good also, or else make the tree evil, and the fruit of it likewise evil.' Matt. xii.

A good man is known by his works: for a good man doth good

works, and an evil man evil works. 'Ye shall know them by their fruit; for a good tree beareth good fruit, and an evil tree evil fruit.' A man is likened to the tree, and his works to the fruit of the tree.

'Beware of the false prophets, which come to you in sheep's clothing, but inwardly they are ravening wolves: ye shall know them by their fruits.' Luke vii.

None of our Works either save us or condemn us.

'If works make us neither righteous nor unrighteous,' then thou wilt say, 'it maketh no matter what we do.' I answer, If thou do evil, it is a sure argument that thou art evil, and wantest faith. If thou do good, it is an argument that thou art good, and hast faith; for a good tree beareth good fruit, and an evil tree evil fruit. Yet good fruit makes not the tree good, nor evil fruit the tree evil; so that man is good ere he do good deeds, and evil ere he do evil deeds.

The man is the tree, his works are the fruit.

Faith maketh the good tree, and incredulity the evil tree: such a tree, such fruit; such a man, such works. For all things that are done in faith, please God, and are good works; and all that are done without faith, displease God, and are evil works.

Whosoever believeth or thinketh to be saved by his works, denieth that Christ is his Saviour, that Christ died for him, and that all things pertain to Christ. For how is he thy Saviour, if thou mightest save thyself by thy works, or whereto should he die for thee, if any works might have saved thee?

What is this to say, Christ died for thee? Verily that thou shouldest have died perpetually; and Christ, to deliver thee from death, died for thee, and changed thy perpetual death into his own death; for thou madest the fault, and he suffered the pain; and that, for the love he had to thee before thou wast born, when thou hadst done neither good nor evil.

Now, seeing he hath paid thy debt, thou needest not, neither canst thou pay it; but shouldst be damned if his blood were not. But since he was punished for thee, thou shalt not be punished.

Finally, He hath delivered thee from thy condemnation and all evil, and desireth nought of thee, but that thou wilt acknowledge what he hath done for thee, and bear it in mind; and that thou wouldst help others for his sake, both in word and deed, even as he hath holpen thee for nought, and without reward.

O how ready would we be to help others, if we knew his goodness and gentleness towards us; he is a good and a gentle Lord, for he doth all for nought. Let us, I beseech you therefore, follow His footsteps, whom all the world ought to praise and worship. Amen!

He that thinketh to be saved by his Works calleth himself Christ.

For he calleth himself the Saviour; which pertaineth to Christ only.

What is a Saviour, but he that saveth? and he saith, I saved myself; which is as much to say as, 'I am Christ;' for Christ only is the Saviour of the world.

We should do no good Works for the intent to get the inheritance of Heaven, or Remission of Sin.

For whosoever believeth to get the inheritance of heaven, or remission of sin, through works, he believeth not to get the same for Christ's sake; and they that believe not that their sins are forgiven them, and that they shall be saved, for Christ's sake, they believe not the gospel: for the gospel saith, 'You shall be saved for Christ's sake;' 'your sins are forgiven for Christ's sake.'

He that believeth not the gospel, believeth not God. So it followeth, that those who believe to be saved by their works, or to get remission of their sins by their own deeds, believe not God, but account him as a liar, and so utterly deny him to be God.

OBJECTION.

Thou wilt say, 'Shall we then do no good deeds?'

ANSWER.

I say not so, but I say we should do no good deeds to the intent to get the inheritance of heaven, or remission of sin: For if we believe to get the inheritance of heaven through good works, than we believe not to get it through the promise of God: or if we think to get remission of our sins by our deeds, then we believe not that they are forgiven us, and so we count God a liar. For God saith, 'Thou shalt have the inheritance of heaven for my Son's sake; thy sins are forgiven thee for my Son's sake:' and you say it is not so, 'But I will win it through my works.'

Thus you see I condemn not good deeds, but I condemn the false trust in any works; for all the works wherein a man putteth any confidence, are therewith poisoned, and become evil. Wherefore thou must do good works, but beware thou do them not to deserve any good through them; for if thou do, thou receivest the good not as the gifts of God, but as debt to thee, and makest thyself fellow with God, because thou wilt take nothing of him for nought. And what needeth he any thing of thine, who giveth all things, and is not the poorer? Therefore do nothing to him, but take of him, for he is a gentle Lord; and with a gladder will giveth us all that we need, than we can take it of him: if then we want aught, let us blame ourselves.

Press not therefore to the inheritance of heaven through presumption of thy good works; for if thou do, thou countest thyself holy, and equal to God, because thou wilt take nothing of him for nought; and so shalt thou fall as Lucifer fell for his pride.

FINIS.

Certain brief Notes or Declarations upon the aforesaid Places of Master Patrick.

This little treatise of Master Patrick's Places, albeit in quantity it be short, yet in effect it comprehendeth matter able to fill large volumes, declaring to us the true doctrine of the law, of the gospel, of faith, and of works, with the nature and properties, and also the difference of the same: which difference is thus to be understood: that in the cause of salvation, and in the office of justifying, these are to be removed and separated asunder, that law from the gospel, and faith from works: otherwise, in the person that is justified, and also in order of doctrine, they ought commonly to go necessarily together.

Therefore, wheresoever any question or doubt ariseth of salvation, or our justifying before God, there the law and all good works must be utterly excluded and stand apart, that grace may appear free, the promise simple, and that faith may stand alone; which faith alone, without law or works, worketh to every man particularly his salvation, through mere promise, and the free grace of God. This word 'particularly,' I add, for the particular certifying of every man's heart, privately and peculiarly, that believeth in Christ. For as the body of Christ is the cause efficient of the redemption of the whole world in general; so is faith the instrumental cause, by which every man applieth the said body of Christ particularly to his own salvation. So that in the action and office of justification, both law and works here be utterly secluded and exempted, as things having nothing to do in this behalf. The reason is this, for seeing that all our redemption universally springeth only from the body of the Son of God crucified, then is there nothing that can stand us in stead, but that only wherewith this body of Christ is apprehended. Now, forasmuch as neither the law nor works, but faith only, is the thing which apprehendeth the body and death of Christ, therefore faith only is that matter which justifieth every soul before God, through the strength of that object which it doth apprehend. For the only object of our faith is the body of Christ, like as the brazen serpent was the only object of the eyes of the Israelites looking, and not of their hands working: by the strength of which object, through the promise of God, immediately proceeded health to the beholders. So the body of Christ, being the object of our faith, striketh righteousness to our souls, not through working, but believing only.

Thus you see how faith, being the only eye of our soul, standeth alone with her object in case of justifying, but yet, nevertheless, in the body she standeth not alone; for besides the eye, there be also hands to work, feet to walk, ears to hear, and other members more, every one convenient for the service of the body, and yet there is none of them all that can see, but only the eye. So in a Christian man's life, and in order of doctrine, there is the law, there is repentance, there is hope, charity, and deeds of charity; all which, in life and in doctrine, are joined, and necessarily do concur together: and yet, in the action of justifying, there is nothing else in man, that hath any part or place, but only faith apprehending the object, which is the body of Christ Jesus for us crucified, in whom consisteth all the worthiness and fulness of our salvation, by faith; that is, by our apprehending and receiving of him: according as it is written in John i., 'Whosoever received him, he gave them power to be made the sons of God, even all such as believed in his name,' &c. Also in Isaiah liii., 'This just servant of mine, in the knowledge of him shall justify many,' &c.

Argument.

Apprehending and receiving of Christ only maketh us justified before God.
Christ only is apprehended and received by faith.
Ergo, faith only maketh us justified before God.

Argument.

Justification cometh only by apprehending and receiving of Christ.
The law and works do nothing pertain to the apprehending of Christ.
Ergo, the law and works pertain nothing to justification.

Argument.

Nothing which is unjust of itself, can justify us before God, or help any thing to our justifying.
Every work we do, is unjust before God.
Ergo, no work that we do, can justify us before God, or help any thing to our justifying.

Argument.

If works could any thing further our justification, then should our works something profit us before God.
No works, do the best we can, do profit us before God.
Ergo, no works that we do, can any thing further our justification.

Argument.

All that we can do with God, is only by Christ.
Our works and merits be not Christ, neither any part of him.

Ergo, our works and merits can do nothing with God.

Argument.

> That which is the cause of condemnation, cannot be the
>   cause of justification.
> The law is the cause of condemnation.
> Ergo, it is not the cause of justification.

A Consequent.

> We are quit and delivered from the law.
> Ergo, we are not quit and delivered by the law.

Forasmuch therefore as the truth of the Scripture, in express words, hath thus included our salvation in faith only, we are enforced necessarily to exclude all other causes and means in our justification, and to make this difference between the law and the gospel, between faith and works; affirming with Scripture and the word of God, that the law condemneth us, our works do not avail us, and that faith in Christ only justifieth us. And this difference and distinction ought diligently to be learned and retained of all Christians; especially in conflict of conscience between the law and the gospel, faith and works, grace and merits, promise and condition, God's free-election and man's free-will: so that the light of the free grace of God in our salvation may appear to all consciences, to the immortal glory of God's holy name. Amen.

The Order and Difference of Places.

The Gospel and the Law;	Faith and Works;
Grace and Merits;	Promise and Condition;
God's Free-Election and Man's Free-Will	

The difference and repugnance of these aforesaid 'Places' being well noted and expended, it shall give no small light to every faithful Christian, both to understand the Scriptures, to judge in cases of conscience, and to reconcile such places in the Old and New Testament as else may seem to repugn; according to the rule of St. Augustine, saying, *'Distingue tempora, et conciliabis Scripturas,'*

&c. 'Make distinction of times, and thou shalt reconcile the Scriptures,' &c. Contrariwise, where men be not perfectly in these places instructed to discern between the law and the gospel, between faith and works, &c., so long they can never rightly establish their minds in the free promises of God's grace, but walk confusedly, without order, in all matters of religion; example whereof we have too much in the Romish church, which, confounding these places together without distinction, following no method, hath perverted the true order of Christian doctrine, and hath obscured the sweet comfort and benefit of the gospel of Christ, not knowing what the true use of the law, nor of the gospel, meaneth.

In the Doctrine of the Law three things to be noted.

In the law therefore, three things are to be considered. First, what is the true rigour and strength of the law, which is, to require full and perfect obedience of the whole man, not only to restrain his outward actions, but also his inward motions and inclinations of will and affection, from the appetite of sin: and therefore saith St. Paul, 'The law is spiritual, but I am carnal,' &c. Whereupon riseth this proposition, That it is not in our nature and power to fulfil the law. Item, the law commandeth that which is to us impossible, &c.

The second thing to be noted in the doctrine of the law, is, to consider the time and place of the law, what they be, and how far they extend. For, as the surging seas have their banks and bars to keep them in, so the law hath its times and limits, which it ought not to pass. If Christ had not come and suffered, the time and dominion of the law had been everlasting: but now, seeing Christ hath come, and hath died in his righteous flesh, the power of the law against our sinful flesh doth cease. 'For the end of the law is Christ;' that is, the death of Christ's body is the death of the law to all that believe in him: so that whosoever repent of their sins, and flee to the death and passion of Christ, the condemnation and time of the law to them are expired. Wherefore this is to be understood as a perpetual rule in the Scripture, that the law with all its sentences and judgments, wheresoever they are written, either in the Old Testament or in the New, doth ever include a privy exception of repentance and belief in Christ, to which al-

94

ways it giveth place, having there its end; and can proceed no further: according as St. Paul doth say, 'The law is our schoolmaster until Christ, that we might be justified by faith.'

Moreover, as the law hath its time how long to reign, so also it hath its proper place, where to reign. By the reign of the law here is meant the condemnation of the law: for as the time of the law ceaseth, when the faith of Christ, in a true repenting heart, beginneth, so hath the law no place in such as be good and faithful; that is, in sinners repenting and amending, but only in them that be evil and wicked. Evil men here I call such as walking in sinful flesh, are not yet driven by earnest repentance to flee to Christ for succour. And therefore saith St. Paul, 'To the just man there is no law set, but to the unjust and disobedient,' &c. By the just man here is meant, not he who never had disease, but he who, knowing his disease, seeketh out the physician; and, being cured, keepeth himself in health, as much as he may, from any more surfeits. Notwithstanding he shall never so keep himself, but that his health (that is, his new obedience) shall always remain frail and imperfect, and shall continually need the physician. Where, by the way, these three things are to be noted; first, the sickness itself: secondly, the knowing of the sickness: thirdly, the physician. The sickness is sin: the knowing of the sickness is repentance, which the law worketh: the physician is Christ. And therefore, although in remission of our sins repentance is joined with faith, yet it is not the dignity or worthiness of repentance, that causeth remission of sins, but only the worthiness of Christ, whom faith only apprehendeth: no more than the feeling of the disease is the cause of health, but only the physician. For else, when a man is cast and condemned by the law, it is not repentance that can save or deserve life, but if his pardon come, then is it the grace of the prince, and not his repentance that saveth.

The third point to be considered in the doctrine of the law, is this: that we mark well the end and purpose why the law is given, which is, not to bring us to salvation, nor to work God's favour, nor to make us good; but rather to declare and convict our wickedness, and to make us feel the danger thereof, to this end and purpose, that we, seeing our condemnation, and being in ourselves confounded, may be driven thereby to have our refuge in Christ the Son of God, and to submit ourselves to him, in whom only is to be found our remedy, and in none other. And this end of the law ought discreetly to be pondered by all Christians: otherwise they that consider not this end and purpose of the law, fall into manifold errors and inconveniences. First, they pervert all order of doctrine: secondly, they seek that in the law which the law cannot give: thirdly, they are not able to comfort themselves, nor others: fourthly, they keep men's souls in an uncertain doubt and dubitation of their salvation: fifthly, they obscure the light of God's grace: sixthly, they are unkind to God's benefits: seventhly, they are injurious to Christ's passion, and enemies to his cross: eighthly, they stop Christian liberty: ninthly, they bereave the church, the spouse of Christ, of her due comfort, as taking away the sun out of the world: tenthly, in all their doings they shoot at a wrong mark; for where Christ only is set up to be apprehended by our faith, and so freely to justify us, they, leaving this justifaction by faith, set up other marks, partly of the law, partly of their own devising, for man to shoot at. And here come in the manifest and manifold absurdities of the bishop of Rome's doctrine, which (the Lord will) we will rehearse, as in a catalogue here following.

Errors and Absurdities of the Papists, touching the Doctrine of the Law and of the Gospel.

1. They erroneously conceive opinion of salvation in the law, which only is to be sought in the faith of Christ, and in no other.

II. They erroneously do seek God's favour by works of the law; not knowing that the law, in this our corrupt nature, worketh only the anger of God.

III. They err also in this, that whereas the office of the law is diverse from, and contrary to the gospel, they, without any difference, confound the one with the other, making the gospel to be a law, and Christ to be a Moses.

IV. They err in dividing the law unskilfully into three parts: into the law natural, the law moral, and the law evangelical.

V. They err again in dividing the law evangelical into precepts and counsels, making the precepts to serve for all men, the counsels to serve only for them that be perfect.

VI. The chief substance of all their teaching and preaching resteth upon the works of the law, as may appear by their religion, which wholly consisteth in men's merits, traditions, laws, canons, decrees, and ceremonies.

VII. In the doctrines of salvation, remission, and justification, either they admix the law equally with the gospel, or else, clean secluding the gospel, they teach and preach the law, so that little mention is made of the faith of Christ, or none at all.

VIII. They err, in thinking that the law of God requireth nothing in us under pain of damnation, but only our obedience in external actions: as for the inward affections and concupiscence, they esteem them but light matters.

IX. They, not knowing the true nature and strength of the law, do erroneously imagine that it is in man's power to fulfill it.

X. They err in thinking it not only to be in man's power to keep the law of God, but also to perform more perfect works than be in God's law commanded; and these they call the works of perfection. And hereof rise the works of supererogation, of satisfaction, of congruity, and condignity, to store up the treasure-house of the pope's church, to be sold out to the people for money.

XI. They err in saying, that the state monastical is more perfect for keeping the counsels of the gospel, than other states be in keeping the law of the gospel.

XII. The counsels of the gospel they call the vows of their religious men, as profound humility, perfect chastity, and wilful poverty.

XIII. They err abominably, in equalling their laws and constitutions with God's law; and in saying, that man's law bindeth, under pain of damnation, no less than God's law.

XIV. They err sinfully, in punishing the transgressors of their laws more sharply than the transgressors of the law of God; as appeareth by their inquisitions, and their canon-law, &c.

XV. Finally they err most horribly in this, that where the free promise of God ascribeth our salvation only to our faith in Christ, excluding works; they, on the contrary, ascribe salvation only, or principally, to works and merits, excluding faith: whereupon ariseth the application of the sacrifice of the mass, *ex opere operato,* for the quick and dead, application of the merits of Christ's passion in bulls, application of the merits of all religious orders, and such others above specified more at large in the former part of this history.

Here follow three Cautions to be observed and avoided in the true understanding of the Law.

The first caution: that we, through the misunderstanding of the Scriptures, do not take the law for the gospel, nor the gospel for the law; but skilfully discern and distinguish the voice of the one, from the voice of the other. Many there be, who, reading the book of the New Testament, do take and understand whatsoever they see contained in the said book, to be only and merely the voice of the gospel: and contrariwise, whatsoever is contained in the compass of the Old Testament (that is, within the law, histories, psalms, and prophets), to be only and merely the word and voice of the law. Wherein many are deceived; for the preaching of the law, and the preaching of the gospel, are mixed together in both the Testaments, as well the Old as the New; neither is the order of these two doctrines to be distinguished by books and leaves, but by the diversity of God's Spirit speaking unto us. For sometimes in the Old Testament God doth comfort, as he comforted Adam, with the voice of the gospel: sometimes also in the New Testament he doth threaten and terrify, as when Christ threatened the Pharisees. In some places again, Moses and the prophets play the Evangelists; insomuch that Jerome doubteth whether he should call Isaiah a prophet or an evangelist. In some places likewise Christ and the apostles supply the part of Moses; and as Christ himself, until his death, was under the law (which law he came not to break, but to fulfil), so his sermons made to the Jews, run all, for the most part, upon the perfect doctrine and works of the law, showing and teaching what we ought to do by the right law of justice, and what danger ensueth in not performing the same: all which places, though they be contained in the book of the New Testament, yet are they to be referred to the doctrine of the law, ever having in them included a privy exception of repentance and faith in Christ Jesus. As for example, where Christ thus preacheth, 'Blessed be they that be pure of heart, for they shall see God,' &c. Again, 'Except ye be made like these children, ye shall not enter,' &c. Item, 'But he that doth the will of my Father, shall enter into the kingdom of heaven,' &c. Item, the parable of the unkind servant, justly cast into prison for not forgiving his fellow, &c. The casting of the rich glutton into hell, &c. with such other places of like condition. All these, I say, pertaining to the doctrine of the law, do ever include in them a secret exception of earnest repentance, and faith in Christ's precious blood. For else, Peter denied, and yet repented. Many publicans and sinners were unkind, unmerciful, and hard-hearted to their fellow-servants; and yet many of them repented, and by faith were saved, &c. The grace of Christ Jesus work in us earnest repentance, and faith in him unfeigned. Amen!

Briefly, to know when the law speaketh, and when the gospel speaketh, and to discern the voice of the one from the voice of the other, this may serve for a note, that when there is any moral work commanded to be done, either for eschewing of punishment, or upon promise of any reward temporal or eternal, or else when any promise is made with condition of any work commanded in the law, there is to be understood the voice of the law. Contrary, where the promise of life and salvation is offered unto us freely, without all our merits, and simply, without any condition annexed of any law, either natural, ceremonial, or moral: all those places, whether they be read in the Old Testament, or in the New, are to be referred to the voice and doctrine of the gospel. And this promise of God, freely made to us by the merits of Jesus Christ, so long before prophesied to us in the Old Testament, and afterwards exhibited in the New Testament, and now requiring nothing but our faith in the Son of God, is called properly the voice of the gospel, and differeth from the voice of the law in this, that it hath no condition adjoined of our meriting, but our respecteth the merits of Christ the Son of God; by whose faith only we are promised of God to be saved and justified: according as we read in Rom. iii. 'The righteousness of God cometh by faith of Jesus Christ, in all, and upon all, that do believe,' &c.

The second caution or danger to be avoided is, that we now, knowing how to discern rightly between the law and the gospel, and having intelligence not to mistake the one for the other, must take heed again that we break not the order between these two, taking and applying the law, where the gospel is to be applied, either to ourselves or towards others. For albeit the law and the gospel many times are to be joined together in order of doctrine, yet the case may fall sometimes, the law must be utterly sequestered from the gospel: as when any person or persons do feel themselves, with the majesty of the law and judgment of God, so terrified and oppressed, and with the burden of their sins overweighed and thrown down into utter discomfort, and almost even to the pit of hell; as happeneth many times to soft and timorous consciences of God's good servants. When such mortified hearts do hear, either in preaching or in reading, any such example or place of the Scripture which pertaineth to the law, let them think the same nothing to belong to them, no more than a mourning weed belongeth to a marriage-feast: and therefore, removing utterly out of their minds all cogitation of the law, of fear, of judgment, and condemnation, let them only set before their eyes the gospel, the sweet comforts of God's promise, free forgiveness of sins in Christ, grace, redemption, liberty, rejoicing, psalms, thanks, singing, and a paradise of spiritual jocundity, and nothing else; thinking thus with themselves, that the law hath done his office in them already, and now must needs give place to his better, that is, must needs give room to Christ the Son of God, who is the lord and master, the fulfiller, and also the finisher of the law; for the end of the law, is Christ.

The third danger to be avoided is, that we do not use or apply on the contrary side, the gospel instead of the law. For as the other before, was even as much as to put on a mourning gown in the feast of a marriage, so is this, but even to cast pearls before swine; wherein is a great abuse among many. For commonly it is seen that these worldly epicures and secure Mammonists, to whom the doctrine of the law doch properly appertain, do receive and apply to themselves most principally the sweet promises of the gospel: and, contrariwise, the other contrite and bruised hearts, to whom belong only the joyful tidings of the gospel, and not the law, for the most part receive and retain to themselves the terrible voice and sentences of the law. Hereby it cometh to pass that many do rejoice where they should mourn; and on the other side, many do fear and mourn where they need not: wherefore, to conclude, in private use of life, let every person discreetly discern between the law and the gospel, and aptly apply to himself that which he seeth convenient.

And again, in public order of doctrine, let every discreet preacher put a difference between the broken heart of the mourning sinner, and the unrepentant worldling, and so conjoin both the law with the gospel, and the gospel with the law, that in throwing down the wicked, ever he spare the weak-hearted; and again, so spare the weak, that he not encourage the ungodly.

And thus much concerning the conjunction and difference between the law and the gospel, upon the occasion of Mr. Patrick's Places.

Notes

Chapter 1. Scotland in the Late Middle Ages

1. For a very insightful examination of Scottish-papal relations see W. Stanford Reid, "The Origins of Anti-papal Legislation in Fifteenth Century Scotland," *Catholic Historical Review* 29 (1943): 445–69. Cf. J. H. Burns, "The Conciliarist Tradition in Scotland," *Scottish Historical Review* 42 (1963): 89–104.

2. Scholarly studies of Wycliffe include John Stacey, *Wyclif and Reform* (Philadelphia: Westminster Press, 1964), and Kenneth B. MacFarlane, *John Wycliffe and English Nonconformity* (London: English Universities Press, 1952). An intriguing and recent popular biography is that by D. G. Fountain, *John Wycliffe: the Dawn of the Reformation* (Sholing, Southampton: Mayflower Christian Books, 1984).

3. Margaret Deansley, *The Lollard Bible* (1920; reprint, Cambridge: The University Press, 1966), and the same author's *The Significance of the Lollard Bible* (London: Athlone Press, University of London, 1951) cover this matter well.

4. W. Stanford Reid, "The Lollards in Pre-Reformation Scotland," *Church History* 11 (1942): 275.

5. Ibid., 272; Alexander MacEwen, *A History of the Church in Scotland* (London: Hodder & Stoughton, 1913), 1:322.

6. *The Original Chronicle of Andrew of Wyntoun*, ed. F. J. Amours (Edinburgh: William Blackwood & Sons, 1906), 3:ix, 100. Cf. John Major, *A History of Greater Britain, as well England as Scotland,* trans. and ed. Archibald Constable, with a *Life of the author* by Aeneas J. G. Mackay (Edinburgh: Scottish Historical Society, 1892), 6:ix, 342.

7. Christopher Anderson, *The Annals of the English Bible*, abridged and continued by S. I. Prime (New York: Robert Carter & Brothers, 1849), 420.

8. J. F. S. Gordon's *Scotichronicon*, as completed by Walter Bower, is the sole source of information about Resby. For a keen analysis of this evidence, see T. M. A. MacNab, "The Beginnings of Lollardy in Scotland," *Records of the Scottish Church History Society* 11 (1953): 254–60.

9. Quoted in T. M. A. MacNab, "Bohemia and the Scottish Lollards," *Records of the Scottish Church History Society* 5 (1935): 15. This article contains a fine summary of the correspondence, with generous quotations.

10. Ibid., 15–16.

11. Alphons Bellesheim, *History of the Catholic Church of Scotland*, ed. and trans. D. O. Hunter Blair (Edinburgh: William Blackwood & Sons, 1887), 2:56. See John Knox, *John Knox's History of the Reformation in Scotland*, ed. William Croft Dickinson (reprint, New York: Philosophical Library, 1950), 1:8–11.

12. Knox, *History* 1:7.

13. *Acts of the Parliaments of Scotland*, vol. 2, 1424–1576 (London: Printed by Command of His Majesty King George the Third, 1814), 7, no. 3.

14. The full text of the papal pronouncement appears in MacEwen, *Church in Scotland* 1:393–95.

15. Knox, *History* 1:8.

16. This is the opinion of MacEwen, *Church in Scotland* 1:383.

17. Knox, *History* 1:8–9. See John Spottiswood, *The History of the Church of Scotland, Beginning in the Year of Our Lord 203, and Continued to the Reign of King James the VI,* with biographical sketch and notes by M. Russell (1665; reprint, Edinburgh: Oliver & Boyd, 1851), 1:120–12. Knox and Spottiswood give slightly varying accounts of these accusations.

18. P. Hume Brown, *History of Scotland* (Cambridge: The University Press, 1902), 1:303.

19. Knox, *History* 1:8.

20. Deansley, *Lollard Bible,* 359.

21. Thomas M. Lindsay, "A Literary Relic of Scottish Lollardy," *Scottish Historical Review* 1 (1904): 260–73), and James Moffat, *The Bible in Scots Literature* (London: Hodder & Stoughton, ca. 1924), contain helpful coverage of the role of the Bible in Lollard endeavors. Nisbet's New Testament is the only surviving piece of Lollard literature from Scotland.

22. See Donald Davidson, "The Influence of the English Printers on the Scottish Reformation," *Records of the Scottish Church History Society* 1(1926): 75–87.

23. James Gairdner, *Lollardy and the Reformation in England* (London: Macmillan & Company, 1908), 2:339 n.3.

24. Anderson, *Annals of the English Bible,* 442.

25. For a succinct account of Tyndale's career and the transmission of his New Testament to the British Isles, see James Edward McGoldrick, *Luther's English Connection* (Milwaukee: Northwestern Publishing House, 1979), 34ff.

26. Moffatt, *Bible in Scots Literature,* 19–20.

27. *Statutes of the Scottish Church, 1225–1559,* trans. 2nd ed. David Patrick (Edinburgh: The University Press, for the Scottish History Society, 1907), 16.

28. Ibid., 262–63.

29. MacEwen, *Church in Scotland* 1:367–68, 410–11.

30. Ibid., 369–70; cf. Ian B. Cowan, "Vicarages and the Cure of Souls in Medieval Scotland," *Records of the Scottish Church History Society* 16 (1969): 111–27.

31. John C. Cunningham, *The Church History of Scotland from the Commencement of the Christian Era to the Present Time* (Edinburgh: James Thin, 1882), 1:160. For poetic criticism from the early sixteenth century see *The Works of Sir David Lindsay of the Mount,* ed. Douglas Hamer (Edinburgh: Scottish Text Society, 1931), 1:3–38.

32. For an extensive account of miracle tales and other superstitions see David Hay Fleming, *The Reformation in Scotland* (London: Hodder & Stoughton, 1910), 137–50.

33. Reid, "Lollards in Pre-Reformation Scotland," 269.

Chapter 2. Scotland in the Renaissance

1. A succinct and very useful account of these matters appears in John Durkan, "The Beginnings of Humanism in Scotland," *Innes Review* 4 (1953): 5–24, a study on which I have relied heavily. Philip E. Hughes, *Lefevre, Pioneer of Ecclesiastical Renewal in France* (Grand Rapids, Mich.: William B. Eerdmans Publishing Company, 1984), is a fresh intellectual biography of great value.

2. *The Letters of James V,* collected and calendared by Robert Kerr Hannay and

edited by Denys Hay (Edinburgh: Her Majesty's Stationery Office, 1954), 167. The character of this king is rather difficult to appraise. Although he may have been a serious Catholic and an enemy of heretics of religious reasons, one interpreter has portrayed him as a cynic interested only in personal gains. See William James Anderson, "Rome and Scotland, 1513–1625," *Innes Review* 10 (1959): 173–93.

3. Ibid., 177–78.

4. This appears in English as *A History of Greater Britain, as well England as Scotland.*

5. See John Durkan, "John Major: After 400 Years," *Innes Review* 1(1950): 131–39, and J. H. Burns, "New Light on John Major," *Innes Review* 5 (1954): 83–97.

6. Major, *History of Greater Britain*, 342.

7. See ibid., Mackay's life of Major, xciii.

8. Ibid., xciv.

9. P. Hume Brown, "Reformation and Scotland," *Cambridge History of English Literature*, ed. A. W. Ward and A. R. Waller (New York: Macmillan Company, 1933), 3:171.

Chapter 3. The Rise of Scottish Protestantism

1. Anderson, *Annals of the English Bible*, 425.

2. Ibid., 428.

3. For the text of this poem see *Works of Sir David Lyndsay*, 1:55–90. The discovery of Lollard elements in this work was made by Thomas M. Lindsay, *A History of the Reformation* (New York: Charles Scribner's Sons, 1907), 2:278.

4. This is the summary of MacEwen, *Church in Scotland* 1:414. *The Dreme* is in *Works of Sir David Lyndsay* 1:3–38.

5. Ibid.

6. For an insightful examination of Scottish Catholicism in the first half of the sixteenth century see W. Stanford Reid, "The Scottish Counter-Reformation before 1560," *Church History* 14 (1945): 104–25.

7. There are documents attesting that 350 children sired by priests were legitimized in the thirty years prior to the Reformation in Scotland. The preponderance of males included in these actions may indicate that the clerics wanted someone to inherit their possessions. Cardinal Beaton had at least eight bastards; Archbishop Hamilton had seven; the bishop of Moray had twelve. Clerical concubinage was practiced openly across Scotland, while canon law prescribed the death penalty for priests who married. See J. D. Mackie, *A History of the Scottish Reformation* (Edinburgh: Church of Scotland Youth Committee, 1960), 80.

8. Peter Lorimer, *Patrick Hamilton, the First Preacher and Martyr of the Scottish Reformation* (Edinburgh: Thomas Constable & Company, 1857), 13.

9. Some helpful studies of this situation include G. G. Coulton, *Scottish Abbeys and Social Life* (Cambridge: The University Press, 1933), and Cowan, "Vicarages and the Cure of Souls," 111–27.

10. See McGoldrick, *Luther's English Connection*, 7.

11. This is the opinion of Alexander F. Mitchell, *The Scottish Reformation*, ed. D. Hay Fleming (Edinburgh: William Blackwood & Sons, 1900), 21.

12. John Strype, *Ecclesiastical Memorials Relating Chiefly to Religion and the Refor-*

mation under King Henry VIII (London: S. Bagster, 1721), 1:568. Cf. McGoldrick, *Luther's English Connection,* 7.

13. *Dr. Martin Luther's Briefe, Sendschreiben* . . . , ed. Wilhelm DeWette (Berlin: Martin Leberecht, 1825–28), 1:25. Copies of the transcript of Luther's debate with John Eck at Leipzig (1519) were circulating in Paris by then, and university scholars were being asked to pass judgment on the disputation. See William Dallman, *Patrick Hamilton: the First Lutheran Preacher and Martyr of Scotland,* rev. ed. (St. Louis: Concordia Publishing House, 1918), 3.

14. N. S. Tjernagel, "Patrick Hamilton: Precursor of the Reformation in Scotland," *Wisconsin Lutheran Quarterly* 74 (1974): 225.

15. See the excellent essay by James Mackinnon, "Patrick Hamilton: Education and Preparation for His Life Work," in *Patrick Hamilton, First Scottish Martyr of the Reformation,* ed. Alexander Cameron (Edinburgh: The Scottish Reformation Society, 1929), 21–27.

16. Lorimer, *Patrick Hamilton,* 53–57.

17. MacEwen, *Church in Scotland* 1:417–18; Lorimer, *Patrick Hamilton,* 60.

18. Ibid., 64. Cf. W. Stanford Reid, "Lutheranism in the Scottish Reformation," *Westminster Theological Journal* 7 (1945): 96.

19. John Howie, *The Scots Worthies,* 2d ed., A. A. Bonar (Glasgow: John McGready, Publisher, [1781]), 5. The arguments of David Laing, editor of Knox's writings, seem persuasive on this. He contended that Patrick Hamilton never took holy orders in the Roman church. See John Knox, *The Works of John Knox* (Edinburgh: James Thin, 1895; reprint, New York: AMS Press, Inc. 1966), vol. 1, 3, 500ff.

20. The list of charges appears in Spottiswoode, *History of the Church of Scotland* 1:124–26.

21. Ibid.; John Foxe, *The Acts and Monuments of the Christian Martyrs,* ed. Stephen Reed Cattley (1843–49; reprint, New York: AMS Press, 1965), 4:559ff.; *Works of Knox* 1:509ff.

22. *John Knox's History of the Reformation in Scotland,* ed. William Croft Dickinson (London: Thomas Nelson & Sons, 1950), 1:11.

23. Lorimer, *Patrick Hamilton,* 88.

24. Tjernagel, "Hamilton: Precursor of the Reformation," 226.

25. The writings of Lambert remain untranslated in Latin editions difficult to find, and the only biography in English is that by Roy Lutz Winters, *Francis Lambert of Avignon (1487–1530): A Study in Reformation Origins* (Philadelphia; United Lutheran Publication House, 1938). Most of the information about Lambert in the present volume comes from Winters. A doctoral dissertation of value is that by Ranier aus Langenselbold Haas, "Franz Lambert und Patrick Hamilton in ihrer Bedeutung für die Evengelische Bewegung auf den Britischen Inseln" (University of Marburg, 1973).

26. For coverage of Lambert's theological development see Winters, *Francis Lambert,* 105–22. Cf. *New Encyclopedia of Religious Knowledge,* s.v. "Francis Lambert," by Carl Mirbt.

27. Foxe, *Acts and Monuments* 4:563. Foxe included the full text of *Patrick's Places;* this treatise also appears, in Knox, *History* 1:219ff.

28. John H. S. Burleigh, *A Church History of Scotland* (London: Oxford University Press, 1960), 121.

29. This is the judgment of Lorimer, *Patrick Hamilton,* 97, and Dallmann, *Patrick Hamilton,* 17. The present author agrees with their position.

30. Martin Luther, *Lectures on Galatians 1535,* ed. and trans. Jaroslav Pelikan, vol. 26 of *Luther's Works* (St. Louis: Concordia Publishing House, 1963), 208–209. Cf. McGoldrick, *Luther's English Connection,* 76–78.

31. Foxe, *Acts and Monuments* 4:563–64.

32. Ibid., 564.

33. Ibid., 565.

34. Ibid.

35. Ibid., 566.

36. Ibid.

37. Ibid., 567.

38. Ibid., 569. Cf. Martin Luther, *The Freedom of a Christian,* trans. W. A. Lambert, rev. Harold J. Grimm, vol. 31 of *Luther's Works* (Philadelphia: Muhlenberg Press, 1957), 333–77.

39. Foxe, *Acts and Monuments* 4:571.

40. Ibid.

41. Martin Luther, *The Bondage of the Will,* trans. J. I. Packer and O. R. Johnston (Westwood, N.J.: Fleming H. Revell Company, 1957).

42. Martin Luther, *Small Catechism* (Philadelphia: General Council Publication Board, 1874), 56.

43. Martin Luther, *Theses Concerning Faith and Law* ed. and trans. Lewis W. Spitz, vol. 34 of *Luther's Works* (Philadelphia: Fortress Press, 1960), 111.

44. See McGoldrick, "Luther on Life without Dichtomony," *Grace Theological Journal* 5 (1984): 3–11.

45. Foxe, *Acts and Monuments* 4:572.

46. For an analysis of revisionist arguments pertaining to Barnes and Tyndale see McGoldrick, *Luther's English Connection,* especially 128–35, and McGoldrick, "Was William Tyndale a Synergist?" *Westminster Theological Journal* 44 (1982): 58–70.

47. Iain R. Torrance, "Patrick Hamilton and John Knox: A Study in the Doctrine of Justification by Faith," *Archive for Reformation History* 65 (1974): 171–85. This article is unclear, and the argument is not supported by anything close to adequate documentation.

48. Lorimer, *Patrick Hamilton,* 125.

49. Robert Lindesay of Piscotie, *The History and Chronicles of Scotland,* ed. Aneas J. G. McKay (1899; reprint, New York: Johnson Reprint Corporation, 1966), 1:308.

50. Ibid., 309.

51. Ibid., 310.

52. Knox, *History* 1:14.

53. Lindesay of Piscottie, *History and Chronicles* 1:310.

54. Cf. ibid., 308:12; Foxe, *Acts and Monuments* 4:559–63; Davide Calderwood, *The History of the Kirk of Scotland,* ed. Thomas Thomson (Edinburgh: The Woodrow Society, 1842), 1:73–76.

55. Lindesay of Piscottie, *History and Chronicles* 1:311.

56. Foxe, *Acts and Monuments* 4:560–61, and Calderwood, *Kirk of Scotland* 1:78–80. Cf. George Buchanan, *The History of Scotland from the Earliest Accounts of that Nation to the Reign of King James VI,* new ed. (Edinburgh: James Kay, 1821), 412–13.

57. Knox, *History* 1:14, and Spottiswoode, *History of the Church of Scotland,* 1:126–27.

58. Spottiswoode, *History of the Church of Scotland* 1:127.

59. Knox, *History* 1–18; Calderwood, *Kirk of Scotland* 1–85:86.

60. J. H. Baxter, "Patrick Hamilton's Martyrdom and the Circumstances of His Time," in *Patrick Hamilton,* ed. Cameron, 19.

61. Lorimer, *Patrick Hamilton,* 159.

62. See McGoldrick, *Luther's English Connection,* 174–76.

63. Lorimer, *Patrick Hamilton*, 217. Some of these figures appear in the next chapter of the present work.

64. Charles C. Butterworth, *The English Primers (1529–1545)* (Philadelphia: University of Pennsylvania Press, 1953), 199–28; for an identification of other Lutheran influences on English Protestantism, see also 279–85.

Chapter 4. Scotland's Earliest Protestants

1. Quoted by Peter Lorimer, *The Scottish Reformation: A Historical Sketch* (New York: Robert Carter & Brothers, 1861),

2. Knox, *History* 1:15.

3. Ibid., 17–18.

4. *Spottiswoode, History of the Church of Scotland* 1:127. Cf. Knox, *History,* in *Works of Knox* 1:19–21, and Calderwood, *Kirk of Scotland* 1:87–93.

5. Foxe, *Acts and Monuments* 5:449, reported that Stephen Gardiner, bishop of Winchester, persuaded Seton to recant his heresies, but Spottiswoode, who reviewed Seton's later writings, denied this. See Spottiswoode, *History of the Church of Scotland* 1:129. Calderwoode, however, accepted Foxe's contention. See his *Kirk of Scotland* 1:93.

6. Calderwoode, *Kirk of Scotland,* 1:92. Since his contemporaries, both Catholic and Protestant, regarded Seton as a preacher of evangelical doctrine, it seems strange that a modern interpreter has written "there is no need to resort to Lutheran teachings to explain the advocacy of reform by friars William Arith and Alexander Seton. . . . They go no further along that road than did John Major" (James K. Cameron, "Aspects of the Lutheran Contribution to the Scottish Reformation, 1528–1552," *Lutheran Theological Journal* [1985]:12).

7. Spottiswoode, *History of the Church of Scotland* 1:129.

8. Ibid.

9. Foxe, *Acts and Monuments* 5:622. Cf. MacEwen, *Church in Scotland* 1:457.

10. Fleming, *Reformation in Scotland,* 190.

11. Anderson, *Annals of the English Bible,* 433 ff., contains extensive coverage of Alesius with helpful excerpts from pertinent documents. See also Lorimer, *Scottish Reformation,* 38–45, and George Mackenzie, *The Lives and Characters of the Most Eminent Writers of the Scots Nation* (1722; reprint, New York: Garland Publishing Company, 1971), 2:144–83. I have drawn heavily from these sources. For Alesius's correspondence with his king see *Letters of James V,* 241 ff.

12. Henry's principal agent in these negotiations was the reformer Robert Barnes, who was striving to win his monarch's support for the reformation of the Church of England. See McGoldrick, *Luther's English Connection,* 16–29.

13. Melanchthon dedicated a new edition of his *Loci Communes* to Henry VIII. See A. F. Scott Pearson, "Alesius and the English Reformation," *Records of the Scottish Church History Society,* 10 (1950): 57–87. This helpful article contains a list of the writings of Alesius, almost all of which have not been translated from Latin. A few excerpts from these works appear as appendixes in Mitchell, *Scottish Reformation,* 295 ff.

14. Bengt Hägglund, *History of Theology,* trans. Gene J. Lund (St. Louis: Concordia Publishing House, 1968), 247–54; Conrad Bergendoff, *The Church of the Lutheran Reformation* (St. Louis: Concordia Publishing House, 1967), 111–13.

15. This matter is covered by J. H. Baxter, "Alesius and Other Reformed Refugees in Germany," *Records of the Scottish Church History Society* 5 (1935): 97–

99, and John T. McNeill, "Alexander Alesius, Scottish Lutheran," *Archive For Reformation History* 55 (1964): 161–91.

16. Gordon Donaldson, "The Example of Denmark in the Scottish Reformation," *Scottish Historical Review* 27 (1948): 57–64, is a succinct treatment of the subject.

17. On MacAlpine see Thorkild Lyby Christensen, "Scots in Denmark in the Sixteenth Century," *Scottish Historical Review* 49(1970):125–40.

18. John Gau, *The Right Way into the Kingdom of Heaven*, ed. A. F. Mitchell (Edinburgh: William Blackwood & Sons for the Scottish Text Society, 1888). The editor has supplied useful biographical and historical data.

19. Ibid., 27–29.

20. Ibid., 25–26.

21. Ibid., 30–31, 75, 107.

22. Ibid., 44 ff.

23. Ibid., 35, 78.

24. Ibid., 62, 80–81.

25. Ibid., 105. See editor's introduction, xxxix.

26. Ibid., XXXV. Mitchell has arranged the passages from Gau and Luther side-by-side. For another example of Scottish dependence on Luther see James K. Cameron, "John Johnsone's *An Comfortable Exhortation of our Mooste Holy Christen Faith and Her Fruites:* An Early Example of Scots Lutheran Piety," in *Reform and Reformation: England and the Continent c. 1500–c. 1750*, ed. Derek Baker (Oxford: Basil Blackwell, 1979), 133–47.

27. Cf. Calderwood, *Kirk of Scotland* 1 : 158, and Hugh Watt, "Henry Balnaves and the Scottish Reformation," *Records of the Scottish Church History Society* 5 (1935): 23.

28. Reid, "Lutheranism in the Scottish Reformation," 101–104.

29. For a succinct account of Wishart's life see Richard Glen Eaves, "George Wishart: His Role in the Scottish Reformation Movement," *Journal of the Alabama Academy of Sciences* 1 (1972): 302–15. Knox gave extensive coverage to Wishart in his *History* 2 : 60 ff. Although Wishart's influence upon Knox was substantial, the latter seems to have absorbed some Lutheran teachings before forming a close relationship with Wishart. There is some reason to believe that Knox taught from Luther's catechism while at St. Andrews Castle in the company of those who killed Beaton. See Hugh Watt, *John Knox in Controversy* (New York: Philosophical Library, 1950), 6–7.

30. David Laing, editor of *Works of Knox*, has shown persuasively that Balnaves was not one of the assassins, although he may have known about the plot prior to the execution of it (*Works of Knox* 3 : 409–10).

31. See Watt, "Balnaves and the Scottish Reformation," 23–39.

32. When Parliament abolished all papal authority it did not establish an ecclesiastical order to replace it but left the reformers to devise their own procedures for the government of the church. When the first general assembly met in December 1560, the ministers and elders present saw the need to establish means to discipline the church in order to maintain purity in doctrine and life. They therefore directed the same reformers who had composed the Confession of Faith to draft a manual of discipline. The commission of reformers eventually presented its document to the general assembly, which approved it after making a few modifications.

The *First Book of Discipline* provided for strict condemnation of behavior that its authors regarded as ungodly, and some members of the royal privy council objected to it. The reformers contended that the new Reformed Church of

107

Scotland should receive the properties of the old Catholic establishment, but many of those holdings had been seized by nobles who refused to relinquish them. Because of aristocratic opposition, Parliament did not approve the *First Book of Discipline.*

Henry Balnaves participated in compiling the *Second Book of Discipline*, which set forth more clearly the relationship of church and state that the reformers desired. It asserted the freedom of the church from state interference, and it, like the *First Book*, called for the return of many church properties. Parliament once again refused to ratify the document. The church, nevertheless, adopted the *Second Book of Discipline* and required all pastors to subscribe to it. By the end of the sixteenth century the government had come to acknowledge the legality of the ecclesiastical system as set forth in the *Second Book of Discipline*, although conflicts between church and state occurred from time to time.

See W. Stanford Reid, "The *Book of Discipline:* Church and State in the Scottish Reformation," *Fides et Historia* 18 (1986): 35–44; James K. Cameron, *The First Book of Discipline* (Edinburgh: The Saint Andrews Press, 1972).

33. This confession, as revised slightly by Knox, appears in *Works of Knox* 3:431–42, where it is preceded by several letters from Balnaves's pen.

34. Ibid. 3:11.

35. For an analysis of Balnaves's debt to Luther see Watt, "Balnaves and the Scottish Reformation."

36. Balnaves, *Confession of Faith*, in *Works of Knox* 3:450.

37. Ibid., 453.

38. Ibid., 459.

39. Ibid., 466.

40. Ibid., 466.

41. Ibid., 466–67.

42. Ibid., 474.

43. Ibid., 492.

44. Ibid., 461.

45. Ibid., 483.

46. Ibid., 476.

47. Ibid., 469.

48. For an analysis of Luther's teaching on this subject see McGoldrick, "Luther on Life without Dichotomy."

49. Balnaves, *Confession of Faith*, 499.

50. Ibid., 497. Tyndale too employed this argument; see McGoldrick, *Luther's English Connection*, 121.

51. Balnaves, *Confession of Faith*, 504. Cf. Luther, *The Freedom of a Christian*, 365.

52. Balnaves, *Confession of Faith*, 518–19.

53. Ibid., 527–30. Cf. Luther, *To the Christian Nobility of the German Nation Concerning the Reform of the Christian Estate, trans* C. M. Jacobs, rev. James Atkinson, vol. 44 of *Luther's Works* (Philadelphia: Fortress Press, 1966), 115–217.

54. Martin Luther, *Lectures on the First Epistle of St. John, trans* W. A. Hansen, vol. 30 of *Luther's Works* (St. Louis: Concordia Publishing House, 1967), 236–37.

55. Balnaves, *Confession of Faith*, 514 (emphasis mine).

56. Ibid., 524.

57. *A Compendious Book of Godly and Spiritual Songs Commonly Known as The Gud and Godlie Ballatis*, ed. A. F. Mitchell (1567; reprint, Edinburgh: William Blackwood & Sons for the Scottish Text Society, 1897), vii–xxiv.

Chapter 5. Conclusion

1. James S. McEwen, *The Faith of John Knox* (Richmond, Va.: John Knox Press, 1961), 22.

2. Richard G. Kyle, *The Mind of John Knox* (Lawrence, Kans.: Coronado Press, 1984), 101.

3. The text of the treatise is in *Works of Knox* 5:7–468.

4. Ibid., 21–30. See McEwen, *Faith of Knox*, 70–71.

5. For this insight the writer is indebted to McEwen, *Faith of Knox*, 56–57. See *Works of Knox* 3:73ff.

6. *Works of Knox* 113; Philip Schaff, *The Creeds of Christendom with a History and Critical Notes* (1919; reprint, Grand Rapids, Mich.: Baker Book House, 1977), 3:467ff.

7. *The Catechism Set forth by Archbishop Hamilton* (Edinburgh: Scottish Text Society, 1882); cf. *The Catechism of John Hamilton*, ed. T. G. Law (Oxford: Oxford University Press, 1884), and Cameron, "Aspects of the Lutheran Contribution," 17–18.

8. *Works of Knox* 4:240.

Annotated Bibliography

Primary Sources

Acts of the Parliaments of Scotland. Vol. 2, 1424–1567. London: Printed by Command of His Majesty King George the Third, 1814. Contains the 1424 law against Lollards.

Andrew of Wyntoun. *The Original Chronicle of Andrew of Wyntoun.* Edited by F. J. Amours. 5 vols. Edinburgh: William Blackwood & Sons, 1906. Important source on Lollardy.

Balnaves, Henry. *The Confession of Faith Concerning How the Troubled Man Should Seek Refuge at His God.* In *Works of John Knox,* vol. 3., edited by David Laing. 1895. Reprint. New York: AMS Press, Inc., 1966. A biblical/theological exposition of justification *sola fide* as it is taught throughout Scripture; shows a debt to Luther but also to Calvin, especially on the doctrine of atonement.

Buchanan, George. *The History of Scotland from the Earliest Accounts of that Nation to the Reign of King James VI.* 3 vols. New ed. Edinburgh: James Kay, 1821. Contains a complimentary reference to Patrick Hamilton but is most useful for the period after his death.

———. *Vernacular Writings of George Buchanan.* Edited by P. Hume Brown. Edinburgh: William Blackwood & Sons for the Scottish Text Society, 1892.

Cowan, I. B., ed. *Blast and Counterblast: Contemporary Writings on the Scottish Reformation.* Edinburgh: The Saltire Society, 1960. Most useful for the period beginning with John Knox.

Foxe, John. *The Acts and Monuments of the Christian Martyrs.* 8 vols. Edited by Stephen Reed Cattley. 1843–49. Reprint. New York: AMS Press, Inc., 1965. Contains *Patrick's Places* and other relevant contemporary documents.

Gau, John. *The Right Way into the Kingdom of Heaven.* Edited by A. F. Mitchell. Edinburgh: William Blackwood & Sons for the Scottish Text Society, 1888. The introduction shows that Gau was indebted heavily to Luther for his understanding of doctrine. *The Right Way* is similar to *Patrick's Plkaces* on law and gospel, and it served as a model for John Hamilton's catechism; written in the Scottish vernacular.

James V. *Letters of James V.* Collected and calendared by Robert Kerr

Hannay and edited by Denys Hay. Edinburgh: Her Majesty's Stationery Office, 1954. Contains letters that document royal policy toward heretics.

Knox, John. *John Knox's History of the Reformation in Scotland.* Edited by William Croft Dickinson. 2 vols. London: Thomas Nelson & Sons, 1950. Knox's account of Patrick Hamilton and other early Scottish Protestants.

————. *The Works of John Knox.* Edited by David Laing. 6 vols. 1895. Reprint. New York: AMS Press, Inc., 1966. Vital source of information about several pivotal figures in addition to Knox himself. Editor's comments are quite valuable.

Lindesay, Robert, of Piscottie. *The History and Chronicles of Scotland, from the Slaughter of King James I to the One Thousand Five Hundredth Three Score Fifteenth Year.* Edited by Aeneas J. G. McKay. 3 vols. 1899. Reprint. New York: Johnson Reprint Corporation, 1966. Contains Patrick Hamilton's confession and a description of his trial.

Lindsay, Sir David. *The Works of Sir David Lindsay of the Mount.* Edited by Douglas Hamer. 2 vols. Edinburgh: The Scottish Text Society, 1931.

Major, John. *A History of Greater Britain, as well England as Scotland.* Archibald Constable, with a *Life of the Author* by Aeneas J. G. McKay. Edinburgh: Scottish Historical Society, 1892. Contains some useful references to Major's hostility toward Lollards and Protestants.

Melville, Sir James. *Memoirs of Sir James Melville of Halhill, 1535–1617.* Edited by A. Francis Steuart. New York: E. P. Dutton & Company, 1930.

Schaff, Philip. *The Creeds of Christendom with a History and Critical Notes.* 3 vols. 1919. Reprint. Grand Rapids: Baker Book House, 1977. "Scots Confession of 1560" appears in this compilation.

Spottiswoode, John. *The History of the Church of Scotland, Beginning in the Year of Our Lord 203, and Continued to the Reign of King James VI,* with biographical sketch and notes by M. Russell. 3 vols. 1665. Reprint. Edinburgh: Oliver & Boyd, 1851. Volume 1 contains important observations and interpretations by the Protestant archbishop of St. Andrews.

Statutes of the Scottish Church, 1225–1559. Translated and edited by David Patrick. Edinburgh: The University Press, for the Scottish History Society, 1907. Documents show conditions in the Roman Catholic church before and during the era of the Reformation; much evidence of clerical ignorance and corruption.

Wedderburn, John, and Robert Wedderburn. *A Compendious Book of Godly and Spiritual Songs Commonly Known as The Gude and Godlie Ballatis.* Edited by A. F. Mitchell. 1567. Reprint. Edinburgh: William Blackwood & Sons for the Scottish Text Society, 1897. Important evidence of Lutheran influences on early Protestant worship in Scotland.

Secondary Sources

Adams, Bruce W. *The Life and Martyrdom of Patrick Hamilton.* Adelaide, Australia: Lutheran Laymen's League, n.d. Brief biographical sketch in pamphlet form.

———. "Patrick Hamilton, a Scottish Lutheran." *The Lutheran* 15 (1981): 467–70, 500–502. Readable and enthusiastic article that extols the subject as an example of courageous faith.

———. "Patrick Hamilton of Scotland, Confessor and Martyr." *The Lutheran* 14 (1980): 510–11. Helpful sketch with bibliographic suggestions.

Anderson, Christopher. *The Annals of the English Bible.* Abridged and continued by S. I. Prime. New York: Robert Carter & Brothers, 1849. Some data about Lollards; extensive excerpts from the writings of Alexander Alesius.

Anderson, William James. "On the Early Career of James Beaton II, Archbishop of Glasgow." *Innes Review* 16 (1965): 221–24.

———. "Rome and Scotland." *Innes Review* 10 (1959): 173–93. Catholic historian's account of corruption in the medieval church; useful for insights into Scottish-papal relations but poorly documented.

Baird, James William. *Thunder over Scotland.* Campbell, Calif.: Green Leaf Press, 1982. Unscholarly life of George Wishart.

Baker, Derek, ed. *Bibliography of the Reform, 1450–1648, Relating to the United Kingdom and Ireland for the Years 1955–70.* Oxford: Basil Blackwell, 1975.

Barnett, T. Ratcliffe. *The Makers of the Kirk.* London: T. N. Foulis, Publisher, 1915. Undocumented and uncritical sketches of numerous Protestant saints; some helpful information about George Buchanan.

Baxter, J. H. "Alesius and Other Reformed Refugees in Germany." *Records of the Scottish Church History Society* 5 (1935): 93–102. Somewhat unclear treatment of Alesius.

Bellesheim, Alphons. *History of the Catholic Church of Scotland.* Edited and translated by D. O. Hunter Blair. 4 vols. Edinburgh: William Blackwood & Sons, 1887. Volume 2 contains useful information about Lollards and Alexander Alesius.

Black, C. Stewart. *The Scottish Church: A Short Study in Ecclesiastical History.* Glasgow: William Maclellan, 1952. This readable survey is marred by numerous errors of fact and dubious interpretations. The author holds historic Protestantism in contempt and maligns it badly.

Bonar, Andrew A. *The Last Days of the Martyrs.* Kilmarnock, Scotland: John Ritchie, LTD., n.d.

Brown, P. Hume. *George Buchanan, Humanist and Reformer.* Edinburgh: David Douglas, 1890. Valuable insights into conditions at the University of Paris while Patrick Hamilton was a student there.

————. *History of Scotland.* 3 vols. Cambridge: The University Press, 1902. Substantial survey.

————. "Reformation and Renaissance in Scotland." In *Cambridge History of English Literature.* Vol. 3, edited by A. W. Ward and A. R. Waller. New York: Macmillan Company, 1933. Survey of principal authors on this era.

Burleigh, John H. S. *A Church History of Scotland.* London: Oxford University Press, 1960. Of some help on Patrick Hamilton.

Burnet, Gilbert. *The History of the Reformation of the Church of England.* Edited by E. Nares. 2 vols. London: Scott and Webster, n.d. Offers only commonplace information about Scotland.

Burns, J. H. "The Conciliarist Tradition in Scotland." *Scottish Historical Review* 42 (1963): 89–104. Shows that Scots supported conciliarism; some useful information about John Major.

————. "New Light on John Major." *Innes Review* 5 (1954): 83–97. Insightful analysis with bibliographic suggestions.

Burton, John Hill. *The History of Scotland.* 3 vols. Edinburgh: William Blackwood, 1867. A little information about James Resby and Patrick Hamilton.

Butterworth, Charles C. *The English Primers (1529–1545).* Philadelphia: University of Pennsylvania Press, 1953. Shows that *Patrick's Places* was incorporated into an early Protestant primer in England; appendix relates Luther's influence on English Protestant literature.

Calderwood, David. *The History of the Kirk of Scotland.* Edited by Thomas Thomson. 4 vols. Edinburgh: The Woodrow Society, 1842. This highly partisan Protestant treatment contains valuable documents from the era.

Cameron, Alexander, ed. *Patrick Hamilton, First Scottish Martyr of the Reformation.* Edinburgh: The Scottish Reformation Society, 1929. Interpretive essays to commemorate the four hundredth anniversary of Patrick Hamilton's death; useful summary and evaluation.

Cameron, James K. "Aspects of the Lutheran Contribution to the Scottish Reformation, 1528–1552." *Lutheran Theological Journal* 19 (1985): 12–20. Well-documented argument that Luther's influence in Scotland was extensive.

————. "Further Information on the Life and Likeness of George Buchanan." *Scottish Historical Review* 42 (1963): 153–42.

————. "John Johnsone's *An Comfortable Exhortation of Our Mooste Holy Christen Faith and Her Fruites:* An Early example of Scots Lutheran Piety." In *Reform and Reformation: England and the Continent c. 1500–c. 1750,* edited by Derek Baker, 133–47. Oxford: Basil Blackwell, 1979. Johnsone witnessed the execution of Patrick Hamilton.

————. "The St. Andrews Lutherans." *St. Mary's College Bulletin* 10 (1968): 17–23. Undocumented account of figures other than Patrick Hamilton.

————, ed. *The First Book of Discipline*. Edinburgh: The Saint Andrews Press, 1972. Editor's extensive introduction and commentary are very important.

Cant, Ronald G. *The College of St. Salvatore*. Edinburgh: Oliver & Boyd, 1950.

Cheyney, Edward P. "The Recantations of the Early Lollards." *American Historical Review* 4 (1899): 423–38.

Christensen, Thorkild Lyby. "Scots in Denmark in the Sixteenth Century." *Scottish Historical Review* 49 (1970): 124–45. Some information about John McAlpine.

Coulton, G. G. *Scottish Abbeys and Social Life*. Cambridge: The University Press, 1933. Many accounts of ecclesiastical corruption in the pre-Reformation era.

Cowan, Ian B. "The Religious and the Cure of Souls in Medieval Scotland." *Records of the Scottish Church History Society* 14 (1963): 215–30. Interesting account of relations between secular and regular clergy.

————. *The Scottish Reformation: Church and Society in Sixteenth Century Scotland*. New York: St. Martin's Press, 1982. Fine examination of political and social developments but weak on theology and roles of particular reformers.

————. "Vicarages and the Cure of Souls in Medieval Scotland." *Records of the Scottish Church History Society* 16 (1969): 11–27.

Cunningham, John. *The Church History of Scotland from the Commencement of the Christian Era to the Present Time*. 2 vols. Edinburgh: James Thin, 1882. Useful for the background for early Scottish Protestantism.

Dallmann, William. *Patrick Hamilton: The First Lutheran Preacher and Martyr of Scotland*. Rev. ed. St. Louis: Concordia Publishing House, 1918. Uncritical sketch.

Davidson, Donald. "The Influence of the English Printers on the Scottish Reformation." *Records of the Scottish Church History Society* 1 (1926): 75–87.

Deansley, Margaret. *The Lollard Bible*. 1920. Reprint. Cambridge: The University Press, 1966. Little about Scotland.

Dickens, A. G. *Lollards and Protestants in the Diocese of York*. Oxford: The University Press, 1959. Nothing on Scotland.

Dickinson, William Croft. *The Scottish Reformation and Its Influence upon Scottish Life and Character*. Edinburgh: St. Andrew Press, 1960.

Donaldson, Gordon. "The Example of Denmark in the Scottish Reformation." *Scottish Historical Review* 27 (1948): 57–64. Compares patterns of reformation in the two countries.

————. *Scotland, James V to James VI*. Edinburgh: Oliver & Boyd, 1971.

Durkan, John. "The Beginnings of Humanism in Scotland." *Innes Review*

4 (1953): 5–24. Shows that Scots were attracted to Erasmus and Lefevre before the introduction of Protestantism.

———. "George Wishart: His Early Life." *Scottish Historical Review* 32 (1953): 98–99.

———. "John Major: After 400 Years." *Innes Review* 1 (1950): 131–39. Historiographic survey of interpretations of Major's role.

Easson, D. E. "The Lollards of Kyle." *The Juridical Review* 10 (1936): 113–28. Critical appraisal of Knox's account, contending that he was accurate in outline but not in details.

Eaves, Richard Glen. "George Wishart: His Role in the Scottish Reformation Movement." *Journal of the Alabama Academy of Sciences* 1 (1972): 302–15. Narrative account with few insights into theological issues; well documented.

———. "Patrick Hamilton: Scotland's First Lutheran Martyr." In *Renaissance Papers*, edited by Dennis G. Donovan and A. Leigh Deneef, 9–16. Printed in Spain for the Southeastern Renaissance Conference, 1972. Brief and readable sketch but one that does little to establish the precise character of the subject's theological position.

Fleming, David Hay. *The Reformation in Scotland.* London: Hodder & Stoughton, 1910. Partisan Protestant treatment with extensive coverage of Patrick Hamilton; a readable classic.

———. *The Scottish Reformation.* 4th ed. Edinburgh: Scottish Reformation Society, 1909. A popular account.

Gairdner, James. *Lollardy and the Reformation in England.* 4 vols. London: Macmillan & Company, 1908–13. Second volume contains a little information about Scotland.

Gordon, J. F. S. *Ecclesiastical Chronicle for Scotland, I, Scotichronicon.* London: James Macveigh, 1875.

Greaves, Richard L. *Theology and Revolution in the Scottish Reformation.* Grand Rapids, Mich.: Christian University Press, 1980. A valuable interpretation of Knox as a political and religious thinker.

Haas, Ranier aus Langenselbold. "Franz Lambert und Patrick Hamilton in ihrer Bedeutung für die Evangelische Bewegung auf den Britischen Inseln." Doctoral dissertation, University of Marburg, 1973.

Hancock, P. D., ed. *A Bibliography of Works Relating to Scotland, 1916–1950.* 2 vols. Edinburgh: The University Press, 1960.

Herkless, John, and Robert Kerr Hannay. *The Archbishops of St. Andrews.* Vol. 3. Edinburgh: William Blackwood & Sons, 1910. A scholarly biography of James Beaton.

Hetherington, W. M. *History of the Church of Scotland.* New York: Robert Carter & Brothers, 1860.

Hewat, Kirkwood. *Makers of the Scottish Church at the Reformation.* Edinburgh: Macniven & Wallace, 1920. Of most use for the period beginning with Knox.

Howie, John. *The Scots Worthies.* 2d ed. of 1781, Edited by A. A. Bonar, Glasgow: John McGready, Publisher, [1781].

Johnston, George. "Scripture in the Scottish Reformation." Part 1, "Historical Statement." *Canadian Journal of Theology* 8 (1962): 249–57. Deals mainly with Knox's use of scripture to justify his program of reform.

———. "Scripture in the Scottish Reformation." Part 2, "Scripture in Public and Private Life of Church and Nation." *Canadian Journal of Theology* 9 (1963): 40–49.

Kyle, Richard G. *The Mind of John Knox.* Lawrence, Kans.: Coronado Press, 1984. A penetrating intellectual biography that compares Knox with other reformers.

Lee, Maurice, Jr. "The Scottish Reformation after 400 Years." *Scottish Historical Review,* 44 (1965): 135–47. Historiographic review.

Lindsay, Thomas M. *A History of the Reformation.* 2 vols. New York: Charles Scribner's Sons, 1907.

———. "A Literary Relic of Scottish Lollardy." *Scottish Historical Review* 1 (1904): 260–73. Important study of Lollardy and its possible connection with Scottish Protestantism.

Linklater, Eric. *The Royal House of Scotland.* London: Sphere Books Limited, 1972. Very useful popular history.

Lorimer, Peter. *Patrick Hamilton, the First Preacher and Martyr of the Scottish Reformation.* Edinburgh: Thomas Constable & Company, 1857. More than a biography, this is a survey of the period surrounding Patrick Hamilton's life; decidedly partisan; well documented; vital primary sources in appendixes.

———. *The Scottish Reformation: A Historical Sketch.* New York: Robert Carter & Brothers, 1861. Useful account of Patrick Hamilton and Alexander Alesius.

McCrie, Thomas. *The Life of Andrew Melville.* 2 vols. Edinburgh: William Blackwood, 1819. Contains information about Lollards and credits them with exerting great influence in Scotland.

———. *Life of John Knox.* 5th ed. Philadelphia: Presbyterian Board of Publication, 1831.

———. *Sketches of Scottish Church History.* 6th ed. Edinburgh: John Johnstone, 1849.

MacEwen, Alexander R. *A History of the Church in Scotland.* 3 vols. London: Hodder & Stoughton, 1913. This substantial survey contains helpful coverage of Lollardy and early Protestantism.

McEwen, James S. *The Faith of John Knox.* Richmond, Va.: John Knox Press, 1961. This beautifully written examination of Knox's doctrine affirms the importance of Luther's influence upon him.

MacFarlane, Leslie J. *William Elphinstone and the Kingdom of Scotland,*

1431–1514: The Struggle for Order. Aberdeen: The University Press, 1985.

McGoldrick, James Edward. "Luther on Life without Dichotomy." *Grace Theological Journal* 5 (1984): 3–11.

———. *Luther's English Connection.* Milwaukee: Northwestern Publishing House, 1979. This examines the lives and beliefs of Robert Barnes and William Tyndale as transmitters of Luther's influence to England.

———. "Patrick Hamilton, Luther's Scottish Disciple." *Sixteenth Century Journal* 17 (1986): 81–88.

———. "Was William Tyndale a Synergist?" *Westminster Theological Journal* 44 (1982): 58–70.

MacIntosh, J. S. *The Breakers of the Yoke: Sketches and Scenes of the Reformation.* Philadelphia: Henry R. Ashmead, 1884.

Mackenzie, George. The Lives and Characters of the Eminent Writers of the Scots Nation. Vol. 2. 1772. Reprint. New York: Garland Publishing Company, 1971. Sketches of several early Scottish reformers.

Mackie, J. D. *A History of the Scottish Reformation.* Edinburgh: Church of Scotland Youth Committee, 1960. Shows Lutheran influences.

MacNab, T. M. A. "The Beginnings of Lollardy in Scotland." *Records of the Scottish Church History Society* 11 (1953): 254–60. A very important article, especially for the role of James Resby.

———. "Bohemia and the Scottish Lollards." *Records of the Scottish Church History Society* 5 (1935): 10–22. A convincing argument for a connection between Lollards of Scotland and Hussites of Bohemia.

McNeill, John T. "Alexander Alesius, Scottish Lutheran." *Archive for Reformation History* 55 (1964): 161–91. A substantial study of a rather obscure figure who ended his life in the camp of the Philippists and probably did not uphold *sola fide.*

McRoberts, David, ed. *Essays on the Scottish Reformation, 1513–1625.* Glasgow: John S. Burns, 1962. This contains some useful interpretations that appeared first in *Innes Review.*

Mitchell, Alexander F. *The Scottish Reformation.* Edited by D. Hay Fleming. Edinburgh: William Blackwood & Sons, 1900. This is an indispensable survey.

Moffatt, James. *The Bible in Scots Literature.* London: Hodder & Stoughton, ca. 1924. Useful coverage of the state of religious knowledge on the eve of the Reformation.

Muller, Gerhard. "Protestant Theology in Scotland and Germany in the Early Days of the Reformation." *Records of the Scottish Church History Society* 22 (1986): 103–17. Deals with Patrick Hamilton chiefly; nothing new.

Pearson, A. F. Scott. "Alesius and the English Reformation." *Records of the Scottish Church History Society* 10 (1950): 57–87. Scholarly biographical

117

essay that portrays its subject as an important influence upon Thomas Cromwell and Thomas Cranmer.

Reid, W. Stanford. "The *Book of Discipline:* Church and State in the Scottish Reformation." *Fides et Historia* 18 (1986): 35–44. A helpful analysis of conditions surrounding composition of this important document.

———. "The Lollards in Pre-Reformation Scotland." *Church History* 11 (1942): 269–83.

———. "Lutheranism in the Scottish Reformation." *Westminster Theological Journal* 7 (1945): 91–111. A concise survey emphasizing that the Reformed leaders built upon Lutheran foundations; rich in bibliographic data.

———. "The Origins of Anti-papal Legislation in Fifteenth Century Scotland." *Catholic Historical Review* 29 (1943): 445–69.

———. "Scotland and the Church Councils of the Fifteenth Century." *Catholic Historical Review* 29 (1943): 1–24. Relates the position of Scotland during the Avignon papacy and the Great Schism.

———. "The Scottish Counter-Reformation before 1560." *Church History* 14 (1945): 104–25. Excellent study of conditions within the Scottish Catholic church during the late Lollard and early Protestant periods.

———. *Trumpeter of God, a Biography of John Knox.* New York: Charles Scribner's Sons, 1974. A thorough account of the reformer's life within the political context of the times.

Rogers, Charles. *Three Scottish Reformers.* London: The Grampian Club, 1876. Contains a chapter on Henry Balnaves.

Ross, Anthony. "Some Scottish Catholic Historians." *Innes Review* 1 (1950): 5–21. Survey of major writers of the Reformation and post-Reformation periods; a little useful information about John Major.

Summers, W. H. *Our Lollard Ancestors.* London: National Council of Evangelical Free Churches, 1904.

Thompson, A. F. *The Later Lollards, 1414–1520.* Oxford: The University Press, 1967. Although this study deals with England primarily, one valuable chapter covers Scotland; the work contains many case histories of heresy.

Tjernagel, N. S. "Patrick Hamilton: Precursor of the Reformation in Scotland." *Wisconsin Lutheran Quarterly* 74 (1974): 222–23.

Torrance, Iain R. "Patrick Hamilton and John Knox: A Study in the Doctrine of Justification by Faith." *Archive for Reformation History* 65 (1974): 171–85. Unclear and unconvincing argument that Hamilton held to a concept of salvation close to the infused righteousness teaching of medieval Scholasticism; poor scholarship.

Trevelyan, George Macauly. *England in the Age of Wycliffe.* New ed. London: Longmans, Green, & Company, 1904.

Watt, Hugh. "Henry Balnaves and the Scottish Reformation." *Records of the Scottish Church History Society* 5 (1935): 23–39. Affirms Luther's influence on Balnaves's doctrine of justification and on early Scottish reformers in general.

———. *John Knox in Controversy.* New York: Philosophical Library, 1950.

Webster, Bruce. *Scotland from the Eleventh Century to 1603.* Ithaca, N.Y.: Cornell University Press, 1975. This historiographic survey of primary sources is, unfortunately, terribly incomplete on ecclesiastical developments.

Whitney, J. P. "Reformation Literature in England." In *Cambridge History of English Literature,* vol. 3, edited by A. W. Ward and A. R. Waller, 28–53. New York: Macmillan Company, 1933. Contains a few details about Murdoch Nisbet and the Scots New Testament.

Winters, Roy Lutz. *Francis Lambert of Avignon (1487–1530): A Study in Reformation Origins.* Philadelphia: United Lutheran Publication House, 1934. Useful account of a little-known teacher of Patrick Hamilton; helpful description of the University of Marburg while Hamilton was there.

Wormald, Jenny. *Court, Kirk, and Community, 1470–1625.* Toronto: The University Press, 1981.

Wright, Ronald Selby, ed. *Fathers of the Kirk.* London: Oxford University Press, 1960.

Index

Alesius (Alane), Alexander: advocacy of vernacular Bible, 59; arrest of, 58; attack on Roman sacramental system, 59; deviation from Luther's teachings, 60; dispute with John Cochlaeus, 59; doctorate from University of Leipzig, 60; relations with Patrick Hamilton, 58; student of John Major, 58; support for Philippists, 60; synergism of, 61; view of Eucharist, 61; at Wittenberg, 58
Andrew of Wyntoun, 16
Arth, William (Friar), 56

Balnaves, Henry: appeal to civil authorities, 68; debt to Martin Luther, 65; employment of biblical theology, 66–67; on extent of the atonement, 68; imprisonment in France, 64; on justification *sola fide*, 65–68; on law and gospel, 66–67; relations with earl of Arran, 63; role in compiling First Book of Discipline, 64; support for militant Protestants, 63–64
Barnes, Robert, 36, 37, 48
Beaton, David (cardinal), 40, 63, 72
Beaton, James (archbishop of Glasgow and St. Andrews), 37, 39–40, 49, 51–52, 56
Buchanan, George, 30, 37

Calvin, John, 53, 60, 61, 64, 71–73
Campbells of Cessnock, 22
Cranmer, Thomas (archbishop of Canterbury), 59
Craw (Crawar), Paul, 18, 19
Cromwell, Thomas, 59

Ecclesiastical corruptions in Scotland, 24–25, 36, 38, 40

Elphinstone, William (bishop of Aberdeen), 25
English Bible, 15–16, 59
Erasmus, Desiderius of Rotterdam, 28, 31, 32, 36–37, 42

First Helvetic Confession of Faith, 70
Folkhyrde, Quentin, 17–18
Foreman, Andrew (archbishop of St. Andrews), 23–24
Forrest, Henry, 57
Foxe, John, 50, 56
Frith, John, 38, 42, 53

Gau, John: exposition of Luther's theology, 62; ministry in Denmark, 61; on salvation, 62; on *sola scriptura*, 62; *Right Way into the Kingdom of Heaven*, 62
Gough, John, 54

Hamilton, John (archbishop of St. Andrews), 72
Hamilton, Patrick: abbot of Ferne, 24, 35, 36; accused of Lutheranism, 39; arrest at St. Andrews, 49–51; on assurance of salvation, 47; Catholic opposition to, 34, 50–51; character of, 35; clerical status of, 38; confession of faith at the stake, 50–51; critic of corruption, 38; execution of, 35; on good works, 48; introduced Luther's teachings into Scotland, 71; on justification *sola fide*, 43; at Marburg, 40, 42; opposition of Archbishop James Beaton to, 49; *Patrick's Places*, 42, 74–100; preaching at St. Andrews, 49; on predestination, 47; return from Germany to Scotland, 49; on sacraments, 53; at

121

University of St. Andrews, 37, 38; at University of Louvain, 36–37; at University of Paris, 36–37; at Wittenberg, 40
Henry VIII (king of England), 29, 33, 56, 59
Huss, John, 18

Indulgences, 19–20, 31

James IV (king of Scotland), 20–21, 22, 27, 29
James V (king of Scotland), 28, 29, 34, 39, 40, 56, 59, 64

Kennedy, James (bishop of St. Andrews), 19
King's College, 27
Knox, John, 19, 20, 40, 55–56, 63–65, 70–73

Lambert, Francis of Avignon: adherence to Lutheranism, 41–42; influence upon Patrick Hamilton, 42; professor at University of Marburg, 41, 42; relations with Ulrich Zwingli, 41, 42; tribute to Patrick Hamilton, 55
Lawrence of Lindores, 17, 18
Lefevre d'Etaples, Jacques, 28, 32
Lindesay, Robert of Piscottie, 49, 50
Lollards, 16–18, 20–21, 22, 25–26, 31, 34
Lorimer, Peter, 35, 38, 40, 49, 53
Luther, Martin: circulation of his ideas in Paris, 37; influence upon Alexander Alesius, 58, 60–61; influence upon Francis Lambert, 41; influence upon Henry Balnaves, 64–65, 67–68; influence upon John Knox, 70–73; influence upon Patrick's Places, 43; John Major's opposition to, 31–32; prohibition of his books in Scotland, 33; on salvation by grace, 47–48, 53
Lutheranism, 26, 31, 53, 56, 70, 73
Lyndsay, Sir David, 34

MacAlpine, John, 62
Major, John: defense of transubstantiation, 31; devotion to Scholas-

ticism, 31–32; Historia Majoris Britanniae, 30; opposition to Lollards, 31; opposition to Lutherans, 31; teacher of Alexander Alesius, 58; at the University of St. Andrews, 30, 37; at the University of Paris, 36
Marburg, University of, 40–41, 42, 55
Melanchthon, Philip, 31, 40, 41, 43, 58, 59, 60

Nisbet, Murdoch, 21

Oxford, University of, 16, 18

Papacy, 13–14, 17, 27, 29, 41, 59
Patrick's Places, 43–47, 54, 74–100
Philip, Prince of Hesse, 40–41, 42, 55

Renaissance humanism, 27–28, 31–32, 37, 38
Resby, James, 17, 18

St. Andrews, city of, 14, 18, 35
St. Andrews, University of, 16, 24, 30, 37–39, 49, 52, 55, 58, 61
St. Leonard's College, 27, 37, 38, 55, 57, 58, 69
St. Salvatore's College, 19, 20, 52, 61, 63
Scots Confession of Faith, 64, 72
Seton, Alexander: adherence to Lutheranism, 56; demand for preaching bishops, 56; on justification sola fide, 57; opposition of Archbishop James Beaton to, 56–57

Torrance, Iain R., 48–49
Tour, M. de la, 33
Transubstantiation, 14, 19–20, 31, 42
Tyndale, William, 21, 22, 34, 37, 42–43, 48, 53, 59

Wedderburn, John, 38, 69, 72
Wedderburn, Robert, 69, 72
Wishart, George, 53, 63, 70
Wolsey, Thomas (cardinal), 33, 60
Wycliffe, John, 14–15, 16–18, 21, 23, 31

Zwingli, Ulrich, 41

About the Author

James Edward McGoldrick has been a professor in the department of history at Cedarville College in Ohio since 1973 and taught previously at John Brown University and West Virginia University. He received his B.S. and M.A. degrees from Temple University and his Ph.D. from West Virginia University. McGoldrick's special interests in teaching and research are British history, the Renaissance and Reformation, and the history of Christianity. He is the author of *Luther's English Connection* (1979), and his published articles have appeared in such periodicals as *Modern Age, The Sixteenth Century Journal, Reformation Today, Westminster Theological Journal,* and *Fides et Historia.* He is a member of the American Society for Church History, the Sixteenth Century Studies Conference, the Society for Scottish Church History, and the North American Conference on British Studies.